Hanging onto
hope

REFLECTIONS AND PRAYERS
FOR FINDING "GOOD"
IN AN IMPERFECT WORLD

MELANNIE SVOBODA, SND

TWENTY-THIRD
PUBLICATIONS
twentythirdpublications.com

DEDICATION

*I dedicate this book to my
grandnieces and grandnephews
who give me hope:
Aaron, Zachary, Cameron Telesz
Rebecca and Marissa Hartman
Ben and Olivia Hartman
Reece and Owen Hartman
Eric Himes
Cody and Andrew Svoboda
Alex and Candice Wicker*

TWENTY-THIRD PUBLICATIONS
A division of Bayard
One Montauk Avenue, Suite 200
New London, CT 06320
(860) 437-3012 or (800) 321-0411
www.twentythirdpublications.com

Cover photo: ©iStockphoto.com/PamelaJoeMcFarlane

ISBN: 978-1-62785-329-3
Library of Congress Control Number: 2017946186
Printed in the U.S.A.

A Division of Bayard, Inc.

Contents

A Scripture scholar was
asked if he could summarize
the Bible in one sentence. He said,
"I can do it in two words:

Life wins!"

Introduction

The French poet Charles Péguy has given us one of the most memorable images of hope. Hope, he says, is a little girl. She is, in fact, the younger sister of Faith and Charity. Hope walks hand in hand with her two taller sisters on the "uphill path" called life. At first, she may appear to be the weakest of the three. But, on the contrary, it is Hope who carries both Faith and Love. It is Hope, says Péguy, "who moves the world."

Péguy's view of the importance and power of hope is not always shared by all Christians. A few years ago, there was a four-day conference on the three theological virtues: faith, hope, and love. The presenters offered to give numerous talks on faith and love, but none of them chose to speak on hope. Eventually, one of the planning committee members volunteered to offer a few thoughts on hope. Closer to home, how many times have you heard sermons on faith and love? Now, compare that to the number of times you have heard sermons on hope. Chances are faith and love win the tally, while hope comes in third. Perhaps a distant third. No wonder some call hope "the forgotten virtue."

Hope can seem to get short-changed even in Scripture. St. Paul's often-quoted hymn to charity ends with these words: "So, faith, hope, and love remain, these three; but the greatest of these is love" (1 Cor 13:13). Such words, as beautiful as they are, could lead some to conclude that hope is second rate. But in other places in Scripture (as we shall see), hope is, in the words of Carroll Stuhlmueller, "the major driving force of life."

When I mentioned to a few friends that I was writing a book on hope, some said, "Good! We need hope now more than ever!" What prompted them to say such a thing? Probably a glance at our headlines. When we turn on the news or open the newspaper, we see stories of war, violence, natural disasters, widespread poverty, political conflicts, critical environmental issues, and injustices of all kinds. Such stories make it easy to conclude that the world is, indeed, falling apart right before our eyes—and we are powerless to do anything about it. In other words, the current national and world situation may seem hopeless.

And it is not only the larger world situation that can seem bleak. Many of us struggle with our personal challenges to hope: loss of a job, financial insecurity, marital infidelity, family conflicts, drug addiction, serious illness, and the death of a loved one. Even our church, once a refuge from despair, has been shaken to the core by scandal. In many places membership is dwindling and deep differences divide some parishes and dioceses.

We can be tempted to lose hope. That is one reason I felt drawn to write this book—not only for others but for myself as well. This book celebrates the importance and power of hope. It explores the virtue of hope from a range of perspectives. It offers definitions, images, and examples of hope in Scripture and today's world. In addition, it explores the relationship between hope and other aspects of our spiritual life such as desire, faith, love, courage, prayer, pain, and sorrow. Each chapter consists of a reflection on the given topic, a short prayer, and questions for personal reflection or group sharing. I firmly believe that music videos can enrich our prayer and reflection. With that in mind, at the end of each chapter I have suggested several music videos that fit the chapter's theme. Virtually all these music videos can be found on YouTube. Just search the song and the artist and the video will come up—sometimes even more than one version.

It is my hope that this book will nourish your hope wherever you find yourself on your spiritual journey. My prayer for all of us is this:

> *May we all hold hands with Hope,*
>   *our "little sister,"*
> *as she helps us to move on the uphill path*
>   *into the future.*
> *May hope bring us ever closer*
> *to the fulfillment of our deepest longings*
>   *and desires:*
> *oneness in love with each other,*
> *and complete union with the life, goodness, beauty,*
>   *and joy of our God.*
> *Amen.*

1

What Is Hope?

In our times, isn't hope the most important virtue?
And the most necessary? And the rarest?
MICHAEL DOWNEY

What exactly is hope? Let's begin with this basic definition: *Hope is a longing or desire for something good in the
future.* Let's break that simple definition apart.

Hope is a *longing* or *desire*. This means that hope is
something that arises inside of us. Hope begins when
we realize there is something we want or need that we
do not have yet. If we were perfectly satisfied with the
way everything was in our personal life and in our world,
then we would have no need for hope—except, perhaps,
to hope that everything would stay exactly the way it was

now—and into the future. But ordinarily hope signifies a deep desire for something in the future that is lacking in the now.

Hope longs for *something good*. Normally, we do not hope for bad things. You did not buy this book saying to yourself, "I hope this book is lousy…I hope it's a waste of money." Or when you are at Mass on Sunday, you are not sitting there thinking, "I hope while I'm here in church, someone steals my car from the parking lot!" No—unless stealing your car would be a good thing for you. Maybe your insurance company would pay you more than it is worth! No, we hope for good things, or at least things we perceive as good.

When writing about hope, St. Thomas Aquinas said that the "something good" we desire is "difficult but possible to attain." In other words, there is no need for hope if the something is easily attainable. Nor is there reason to hope if the something is completely beyond our grasp. At my age and physical condition, for example, there is no reason for me to hope to win an Olympic gold medal in weightlifting!

Hope longs for something good *in the future*. And here's the rub: nobody knows the future. Nobody. That's one reason we buy insurance—to protect ourselves against a possible future mishap or catastrophe such as a car accident, a house fire, serious illness, and even death. Insurance companies make their money based on the fact that the future is the great unknown. As such, it can be a very scary place.

Yes, we can observe trends and make some predictions about the future. And sometimes our predictions are right. But not always. The tearing down of the Berlin Wall was not predicted. In fact, it came as a surprise to many people—even those serving in intelligence agencies around the world. The outcomes of some presidential elections are not always what the pollsters predict either. And what about the world of sports? Ordinarily we can predict that a superior team will defeat an inferior one. But sports fans know that on any given day, even a lousy team can beat a great team. That is one reason sports can be so exciting: Nobody *really* knows the outcome of the game. So, if you are a devoted fan of a lousy team (as I am sometimes), then you get a lot of exercise in hoping!

What are some of the implications of all of this for our Christian living? First, this definition of hope underscores the importance of desire in our life. Too often in the past, as we shall see, our tradition of Christian spirituality taught us to look with suspicion upon our desires and longings. Yet it is precisely through the deepest yearnings of our heart that God speaks to us and directs us. It is crucial to be in touch with these longings, because hope is rooted in them; hope springs from them. In this regard, I recall the famous guru who said to his students:

"The enlightenment you seek is already in you." We could paraphrase: "The hope you seek is already in you. It is residing in the deepest longings of your heart."

This definition of hope also raises several important questions. What is truly good? Is the good we are hoping for, good only for me? Or is it good for others as well? Later in this book we will explore the essential communal dimension of hope.

A third implication is this: We live in an imperfect world. Hope acknowledges this fact. For, what we essentially hope for is a better world, a more perfect world. As Péguy said in his poem, Hope is the virtue that *carries* Faith and Charity. Hope is the virtue that generates our concrete actions to make the world a better place, while whispering in our hearts, "A better world is possible." Or, as Jesus said, "The Kingdom of God is at hand" (Lk 10:9).

We also might be asking: Where does hope come from? To whom is it ultimately directed? For Christians, the answer to both of those questions is, of course, God. For it is God who plants these deepest longings in our heart, longings that can be filled only by our complete oneness with God.

Finally, all of this raises another question—perhaps the most significant one of all: In what or in whom do we place our hope? As we shall see, the answer to that question makes all the difference in the world.

God of my deepest longings and desires,
* keep the flame of hope alive in my heart.*
Make me attentive to what is lacking
* in my personal life and*
* in the larger world.*
Give me a view of the future
* that sees not desolation,*
* but possibility.*
Keep whispering in my heart,
* "A better world is possible."*
Give me the grace to partner with you,
* with Jesus, and with the Holy Spirit*
to help make that better world a reality.
Amen.

REFLECTIVE QUESTIONS

1. To what extent do you agree or disagree with Michael Downey's quote at the beginning of this chapter?

2. What is your basic attitude toward the future? Do you see it as a place of desolation or possibility?

SUGGESTED MUSIC VIDEOS

- "On Eagle's Wings," Michael Joncas
- "All Is Gift," Kathleen Sherman
- "Amazing Grace," Il Divo at the Coliseum

2

Longings and Desires

Here, in this life, all symphonies remain unfinished.

KARL RAHNER, SJ

Hope is rooted in our deepest longings and desires. Hope begins with the awareness that we are not yet fulfilled—no matter how successful we may be or how many items we have checked off our bucket list. Like little Oliver Twist, we are holding out our empty bowl and pleading with the powers-that-be, "More! More!" Centuries ago, St. Augustine penned those timeless words describing this innate discontent: "Our hearts are restless, Lord, until they rest in Thee." People of hope have experienced this deep-seated restlessness. They are in touch with their deep longings and desires.

But, as I mentioned earlier, longings and desires are sometimes viewed negatively in our Christian tradition. In the words of Father James Martin, SJ, longings and desires "get a bad rap in many spiritual circles." Sometimes they are equated with sexual desire or material wants.

Scripture, however, gives us essentially two views of desire: Desire as dangerous and desire as holy. Eve desired the apple, David desired Bathsheba, the religious leaders desired to silence Jesus. Those are examples of desire as dangerous, desire that led to sin and evil. But desire can also be holy. Moses desired to free his people from slavery, Mary desired to be the handmaiden of the Lord, and Paul desired to spread the Good News to the Gentiles. Their desires led to goodness and new life.

This means we have to sort out our desires to see if they spring from God and love, or if they rise from lesser things such as fear, envy, selfishness, or laziness. We must also differentiate between surface desires and desires that rise from the depths of who we are. Surface desires are desires such as these: "I have a craving for pizza" or "I wish it would rain (or stop raining)" or "I'd like to make more money." If we trace such desires to their roots, we might eventually find a deeper desire. The desire for more money, for example, might really flow from the deeper desire for security or the desire to be loved and appreciated.

Sometimes we may need help with getting in touch with our deeper desires. A good friend or spiritual director can aid us in this endeavor. We can begin by pondering questions such as these: What do I *really* want in life? Are there any changes I would like to make in the way I am living my life? What gives me comfort and courage? What frightens me? How am I experiencing love in my life? What is my dream for myself, my family, and humankind?

Desire is a vital component of our spiritual life because it is a key way God speaks to us. How important it is, then, to keep our deepest desires alive. Many of the saints spoke about the necessity of fostering "holy desires." St. Augustine said, when we do not have time for formal prayer, then "the desire of your heart is itself your prayer." St. Teresa of Ávila said that the fostering of holy desires begins with acknowledging God's presence in our heart. St. Teresa wrote: "We have only to find a place where we can be alone to look upon him present within us. Nor need we feel strange in the presence of so kind a Guest."

St. Ignatius, too, stressed the importance of desire in the spiritual life. In fact, one of the stated purposes of his Spiritual Exercises was this: "to find better what I desire." Ignatius believed that God uses our deep desires to communicate God's desire for us. Consequently, our desires can lead us to become the person God is calling us to be.

Ignatius also encouraged a practice that some have called "holy daydreaming." On a regular basis, Ignatius took time to picture himself undertaking difficult and wonderful deeds for God. This was one way he kept his desires—and hope—alive in his heart.

There is a beautiful story in the Gospel of Mark that shows Jesus encouraging someone to know and name his desires. It is the story of the cure of Bartimaeus, the blind man (10:46–52). Bartimaeus is on the side of the road begging when he hears a commotion. He learns that Jesus is passing by. Immediately, Bartimaeus calls out to Jesus, "Son of David, have pity on me." The crowd tries to quiet him, but he keeps yelling out. Finally, Jesus stops and calls to Bartimaeus. The blind man throws off his cloak and runs to Jesus. And what does Jesus say? He asks, "What do you want me to do for you?" Jesus is asking Bartimaeus to articulate his deep desire. And Bartimaeus says, "Master, I want to see."

Jesus asks us that same question when we come to prayer: "What do you want me to do for you?" He invites us to name our deep desires. Some of the Psalms capture beautifully the essence of our desire: our longing for God. Here are excerpts from two such psalms. I suggest you read these lines aloud and slowly, trying to make the words your own:

> As the deer longs for streams of water,
> So my soul longs for you, O God.
> My being thirsts for God, the living God.
> When can I go and see the face of God?
> (Ps 42:2–3)

> O God, you are my God—
> For you I long!
> For you my body yearns;
> For you my soul thirsts,
> Like a land parched, lifeless,
> And without water. (Ps 63:2)

> *God of my deepest longings and desires,*
> *   with St. Augustine I say,*
> *"My heart is restless until it rests in Thee."*
> *Help me to acknowledge my incompleteness,*
> *   my discontent, my lack of fulfillment.*
> *Then help me to name and articulate*
> *   my deepest longings and desires,*
> *for it is through them that you are speaking to me*
> *and directing my life.*

Help me to make these words my own:
  "O God, you are my God—
  For you I long!
  For you my body yearns;
  for you my soul thirsts."
Amen.

REFLECTIVE QUESTIONS

1. If Jesus appeared to you today and asked, "What do you want me to do for you?" How would you answer his question?

2. What are some ways you can discern whether a desire is from God or from some lesser thing such as fear, envy, or selfishness?

SUGGESTED MUSIC VIDEOS

*   "As the Deer," Praise and Worship Songs
*   "Be Thou My Vision," Celtic Woman
*   "O God, You Search Me and You Know Me," Bernadette Farrell

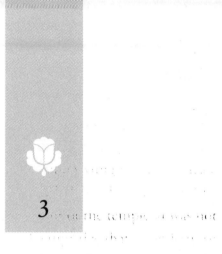

3

Hope and the Imperfect World

The ability to live joyfully in an imperfect world is a sign of Christian maturity. **RICHARD ROHR**

Hope is not naive optimism. Optimists see the world through so-called rose-colored glasses, that is, they see one part of life, the sunny side. Or if you prefer another image, they see the roses and not the thorns. Some might think that optimists are the opposite of pessimists. But in reality, they are similar—except that pessimists view life through gray-colored glasses. They see the thorns and not the roses.

Both optimists and pessimists focus on only part of reality, the obvious good or the obvious bad. They fail to see any middle ground or the ambiguous. The ambiguous is that part of life that is not clearly good or clearly bad, not clearly right or clearly wrong, but rather a mixture. Hope, in contrast to optimism and pessimism, sees a wider view of reality: the good, the bad, and the ambiguous. Years ago I had a Scripture professor at Duquesne University named Fr. Demetrius Dumm, OSB. I can still remember him saying with great gusto one day in class, "Sooner or later in life you have to learn to deal with ambiguity, because life is 70% ambiguous."

Hope, then, knows how to deal with ambiguity. In fact, it can find the good in the ambiguous. But hope goes even further than that. Hope can detect the good even in the apparently bad. An old story might illustrate this point. A little boy wanted a pony in the worst way. He hoped and hoped that he would get one for his birthday. His parents began to grow weary of his hopeful, upbeat attitude, so they played a little trick on him. The morning of his birthday they told him to go out into the small barn and he would find his pony. The boy ran to the barn, but when he got there, he saw only a huge pile of manure in the stall. The pile was taller than he was! The parents expected the boy to return to the house totally dejected. But when he didn't come back right away, his parents went out to investigate. There was the boy, cheerfully shoveling the manure. "What are you doing?" his parents asked. "I'm shoveling!" he said with great enthusiasm. "I figure with all this manure, there's gotta be a pony in here somewhere!" Hope longs for a pony. But hope realizes it might have to shovel a lot of manure to find that pony!

Hopeful Christians who are mature in their faith have embraced the imperfect world. They know that life comes to us with a great deal of ambivalence. We see this ambivalence in individuals, families, social movements, government, the church. As we grow in self-knowledge, we realize we too are a mixture of idealism and pettiness, generosity and selfishness, eagerness and laziness, thoughtfulness and insensitivity. Hope sees this mixed bag and is not disheartened.

That is why hope is stronger than mere optimism. In his book *Hope Without Optimism*, Terry Eagleton writes that optimism "is chained to cheerfulness" and thus lacks the "strenuous commitment" that is essential to hope. Hope is a strong virtue rooted in reality. For it knows that it is only in the real world that we encounter God. As writer Frederica Matthewes-Green has said, "Reality is God's home address."

Furthermore, hope believes that whatever happens in

life, whatever twists or turns our journey may take, whatever valleys or mountains we may have to negotiate, God is present in it all. Even more, hope believes that God is bringing about good even from seemingly unpromising or even negative situations.

Hope is a gift. It is the gift God bestows on us so we may continuously seek God and grow in goodness, love, and happiness. But hope demands a response on our part. Hope is not simply a feeling. It is a choice; it is a decision. We choose to hope not because we are blind to the evils in the world, but because we have a vision that goes beyond the immediate or the readily visible. Our faith in God and in Jesus tells us that God's grace is at work just beneath the surface of the observable, transforming the world into the Reign of God.

Blaise Pascal said that faith is a wise wager. I think hope is a wise wager too. As Christians we hope, that is, we are betting *with our whole life* that our deepest longings are leading us to God. We are betting that no matter how messy or confused our lives may be, God is with us extracting good from the very stuff of our every day. We are betting that good will triumph over evil, love is stronger than hate, and death leads to everlasting life. And we are making such a wise bet because we believe in the promises of God and the life and teachings of Jesus.

When we hope, we are betting that a better world is coming. It is already in process. The Indian human rights activist Arundhati Roy is a woman of hope working for a better tomorrow. She writes: "Not only is another world possible, she is on her way. On a quiet day, I can hear her breathing."

> *God of hope,*
> *help me to live joyfully in the imperfect world,*
> *the world of the good, the bad, and the ambiguous.*
> *May I live in this real world with enthusiasm,*
> *and not become disheartened*
> *by some of the negative things I see and experience.*
> *May I daily choose to have hope because*
>   *I have a vision*
> *that goes beyond the immediate or the*
>   *readily visible.*
> *May I bet with my whole life that a better world*
>   *is not only possible,*
> *she is on her way.*
> *Give me the quiet grace to hear her breathing.*
> *Amen.*

REFLECTIVE QUESTIONS

1. To what extent do you agree or disagree with this statement: "It is only in the real world that we encounter God"?

2. Have you ever experienced God bringing good from an apparent evil? Or bringing good from the very "stuff of your life"?

SUGGESTED MUSIC VIDEOS

- "Come as You Are," David Crowder
- "In His Time," Maranatha! Singers
- "Change My Heart, O God," Vineyard

4

Challenges to Hope

By sharing in the holy communion of trouble,
we become bonded more tightly together as members
of one great family. **FATHER EDWARD HAYS**

A woman met a man on the street who looked destitute. She slipped a dollar into his hand and whispered, "Never despair." A few days later, the man met the woman and slipped nine dollars into her hand. "Here's your winnings," he whispered. "My winnings?" she asked. The man was a bookie. The horse "Never Despair" came in first, paying 8 to 1!

Never despair. Easier said than done, we say. For of all the challenges to hope, despair is the ultimate one. In fact, the word despair is even defined as "the complete absence of hope." As we also know, in Dante's *The Divine Comedy*, the inscription at the entrance to Hell reads, "Abandon hope, all ye who enter here." Despair, according to Dante, is the essence of Hell.

There are other challenges to hope that are more subtle than outright despair. The first one is cynicism. Someone has said that a cynic is a person who is prematurely disappointed in the future. Cynics believe that people are basically selfish and dishonest. They believe that things will never get any better—no matter what. So, the good you are trying to do, forget it… It won't work… Been there, done that… Nothing's going to change. What the cynic is really saying is: No better world is possible.

We meet cynics wherever we go. Let's say you are attending a brainstorming session at your parish to try to come up with some ways to get parishioners to take a more active role. Someone offers a suggestion. As soon as the words are out of her mouth, the cynic in the group will bellow, "It'll never work!" Or "We tried that already!" Or "People will never go for that!" Or "What's the use?" In saying such things, cynics deny we are on any kind of journey. They deny the human potential for generosity and personal transformation. They deny that God can do great things in and through us. If we are honest, we have to admit that we are probably cynical at times too.

A few years back, Honest Tea, Inc., conducted an unscientific study to gauge how honest or dishonest Americans were. They put out bottles of their tea in twenty-seven U.S. cities and sold them for one dollar each, waiting to see if people would pay for the tea on the "honor system." They sold thousands of bottles and concluded that 94% of Americans were honest. The top city was Atlanta with a 100% honesty rate! A few years later they repeated the experiment—maybe to see if the results of the first experiment were a fluke. And guess what? The second test concluded that 93% of Americans were honest. The top cities that year were Honolulu and Austin. The point is we humans may be more honest than we give ourselves credit for.

Another challenge to hope is busyness. If we are constantly busy with a zillion things to do, chances are we will not have the time necessary to get in touch with those deeper longings of our heart. And, as we already saw, it is precisely in these longings that hope is born. Excessive speed is another challenge to hope. In her book *Altar in the World*, Barbara Brown Taylor writes, "Most of us move so quickly that our surroundings become no more than the blurred scenery we fly past on our way to somewhere else." If we are rushing helter-skelter from place to place, we might fail to be aware of the deeper and more significant movement called "the journey of our life." Hope does not stand much of a chance if we have 1,001 things on our "To Do" list—unless we put on that list something like this: "Meet with God today and talk about my dreams."

Our culture places significant demands on us. Yes, it is true we have many so-called labor saving devices, such as instant food, rapid transit, and high speed internet. But what are we doing with all the time we are supposedly saving? Sometimes I think we just keep increasing our workload. (If I made twenty-five widgets today, then I'll try to make thirty tomorrow!) Or we keep increasing our speed. (If I cooked a complete meal in twenty-seven minutes today, then maybe tomorrow I can do it in twenty-two!)

Anne Lamott offers two activities to help us from getting overwhelmed by our busy and fast-paced world: rest and laughter. Both activities can also nourish our hope. As Christians, we can rest regularly because we know we do not have to be God. As Rev. Joan Brown Campbell reminds us, "That job is already taken." And we can laugh regularly too. With hope we are freed from taking everything—including ourselves—too seriously. Hope frees us from the kind of fear and worry that sucks the joy out of daily living.

Hope is not easy. There's a little story that illustrates this point. One Victorian-era funeral parlor used to advertise: "For composing the features, $1. For giving the features a look of quiet resignation, $2. For giving the features the appearance of Christian hope, $5." The challenges to hope are many and real. But we believers know hope's origin. And we know hope's destiny. That origin and destiny is a Person, is God. And, in the words of G.K. Chesterton, our God "loves us furiously."

God of furious love,
help me to meet the challenges to hope.
Help me to reject all cynicism.
Instead of my asking, "What's the use?"
* teach me to ask, "Why not?"*
Help me to make wise choices
* about all the things I have to do.*
Discourage me from putting unrealistic demands
* upon myself.*
Encourage me even to say "no" at times.
God of Hope, slow me down.
Invite me to rest.
Help me to bring more laughter into my life.
I ask for these things from you,
* my Origin and my Destiny.*
Amen.

REFLECTIVE QUESTIONS

1. What is one of the greatest challenges to your hope? What helps you to face this challenge?
2. How do you incorporate rest and laughter into your life?

SUGGESTED MUSIC VIDEOS

- "Breathe," Jonny Diaz
- "Be Still My Soul," Kari Jobe
- "Make Me a Channel of Your Peace," Susan Boyle or Angelina (EWTN)

5

In Whom Do We Hope?

Creation's Response

*Ah, gentle God, if thou art so lovely in thy creatures,
how exceedingly beautiful and ravishing
thou must be in thyself.* **BLESSED HENRY SUSO**

Earlier I said that one of the most important questions
we can ask is this: *in whom* do we hope? For Christians,
the answer of course is God. But that answer leads to

another question: who is God? What follows is a response to that question as gleaned from creation. The next chapter will respond to that question using Scripture. Let's begin here with the world of nature.

Fr. Thomas Berry, an ecotheologian, called creation "the first scriptures." Long before the Bible was written, God was revealing God's self through the natural world. Berry believed we can learn many things about the Creator by observing and reflecting on creation. What things?

First, the wonder of existence itself. Why is there anything at all let alone the beauty and mystery that is all around us and inside of us? Why stars, why earth, why oceans, why trees, why whales, why butterflies, why lilacs, why strawberries, why amoebas? Why anything? Why me?

We can never answer that question completely, of course. But Evelyn Underhill, the English mystic, suggests that all of creation springs "from an ardor, an immeasurable love, a perpetual donation, that generates, upholds, and drives it." Everything, she maintained, is "enwrapped in love, not by mechanical necessity, but by God's passionate desire." Existence itself gives us a glimpse of God's ardor, God's drive, God's passion.

What else might we learn about the Creator from creation? Let us consider size. What is big and what is small? It all depends. Consider our solar system. Let's start with the sun. It is large. Quite large. In fact, a million earths could fit inside our sun. Yet another star labeled *vy canis majoris* is two thousand times wider than our sun. Returning to our solar system, did you know that you have never seen our solar system drawn to scale? Why not? Because it is far too expansive. If earth were the size of a pea, for example, Jupiter would be one thousand feet away. Pluto would be a mile and a half away.

Let's talk about stars. As we know, light travels 186,000 miles per second. Yet the light from our nearest star takes almost five years to reach planet earth. Other stars are much, much, much farther away—1,000 light years away or 10,000 or 100,000. The Hubble telescope has enabled us to see farther and farther into the universe. One of my favorite pictures taken by Hubble is of the beautiful sombrero galaxy that is 28 million light years away! To say that the universe is humongous is an understatement! When we contemplate the sheer size of our universe, we wonder: What must the Creator God be like?

Now let's go the other way. We all know that atoms, the building blocks of the universe, are very small. But how small? Here's how small. If half a million of them lined up side by side they could hide behind a human hair. Subatomic particles are even tinier. And guess what, they are all moving. From the most distant galaxies to inside our brains, these subatomic particles are racing at 40,000 miles per second! That's 14 million miles per hour!

So movement is another intrinsic trait of creation. If you are sitting in a chair and reading this, you may think you are stationary. But, because the earth is rotating, you are being hurled eastward at about 750-1000 miles per hour (depending on how close to the equator your are). Simultaneously you are revolving around the sun at 67,000 miles per hour. Unbelievable! We do not feel this movement, of course, because we're moving too, and because our atmosphere and everything else moves right along with us.

That's size, the gigantic and the infinitesimal. Now let's look at life on our planet. What were the chances of life appearing on earth? Astronomers and astrobiologists say the chances of life appearing on earth are not a million-to-one or even a billion-to-one, but something much higher. We are extremely, extremely, extremely fortunate and blessed that all the conditions on earth were just right and all the building blocks were present to enable life to appear—and survive. What does that tell you about our Creator God?

And when we look around at all the forms of life on this planet, aren't we amazed at the incredible variety we behold? We see birds of all kinds from tiny hummingbirds to gigantic condors. We see elephants, tigers, giraffes, whales, anteaters, polar bears, goats, cats, dogs, horses, squirrels, and the list goes on. There are one and a half million species of animals on earth. There are 950,000 species of insects. And over 26,000 species of orchids! The Creator is astoundingly creative. There seems to be no limit to God's imagination, God's genius, God's yearning for diversity. St. Gregory of Nyssa wrote these words back in the fourth century—long before we had telescopes or microscopes. Yet his words still ring true: "The Divine is present in everything, pervading and penetrating it."

This chapter is filled with superlatives and exclamation points. How could we write about creation without being drawn to say, Wow! Our God is indeed an awesome God! In the words of Fr. William O'Malley, SJ: "Something exhilarating could happen to your living if you ever owned the truth that the Unspeakably Holy One, The Architect of infinite quasars and infinitesimal quanta—the Ultimate Wow—knows your name, calls you his, finds you precious." And this leads us to the next chapter where we ponder the God who is revealed to us in Scripture.

Creating God,
when I gaze at the stars at night,
when I stand beside the ocean,
when I view the mountains in the distance,
I cannot help but say:

You are an awesome God!
When I behold the diversity of the animal world,
the fruit of your endless imagination,
and when I contemplate atoms and galaxies,
I cannot help but say:
You are an awesome God!
Help me to trust your creativity,
*   your genius, and the power of your passion.*
Give me the grace to draw near to you.
Give me the grace to trust you.
Give me the grace to place all my hope in you.
Amen.

REFLECTIVE QUESTIONS

1. What does nature reveal to you about God?
2. What role does creation play in your daily life? In your spiritual life?

SUGGESTED MUSIC VIDEOS

- "Everything Is Holy Now," Peter Mayer
- "How Great Thou Art," Chris Rice
- "Creation Calls," Brian Doerksen

6

In Whom Do We Hope?

Scripture's Response

The primary purpose of reading the Bible is not to know the Bible but to know God.

JAMES MERRITT

In the previous chapter, we reflected on nature's response to the question: Who is God? In this chapter we will explore that question using Scripture.

Who is God? Scripture answers that question in a

number of ways. When Moses encounters God in the burning bush, God says, "I have witnessed the affliction of my people in Egypt and have heard their cry of complaint against their slave drivers, so I know well what they are suffering. Therefore I have come down to rescue them" (Ex 3:7–8). What do we learn from these words?

First, we learn that God hears our human cries of pain and is moved to compassion by them. Next, God's compassion prompts God to take action. God appears in the burning bush and actually speaks to Moses. God takes the initiative in communicating with humans. We also learn that God is interested in human affairs and is somehow involved in them. God then reveals his desire to Moses: to rescue the Israelites from slavery. We can deduce from this desire that one of God's top priorities for humans is freedom. Then God asks Moses to lead the people out of Egypt. God solicits human help to achieve this goal of freedom. And finally, God promises to be with Moses and with the people throughout the process of liberation.

Later when God speaks to Moses in the desert, God says these words that reveal even more about who God is: I am "merciful and gracious, slow to anger, and abounding in steadfast love" (Ex 34:6). God is merciful and gracious; therefore, we need not fear to approach this God. God is abounding in steadfast love. I especially appreciate that phrase *steadfast love*. *Steadfast love* connotes loyalty, faithfulness, and constancy. Our hope, then, is anchored in this steadfast love of God.

This steadfast love of God is shown throughout the Old Testament. God enters into a covenant with the Israelites. God gives them the Ten Commandments to guide them toward greater freedom and happiness. Although the Israelites were unfaithful to God repeatedly, God remained faithful to them, forgiving them again and again. God promises to send them a Messiah, someone who will come in the future to redeem God's people from the slavery of sin and establish the Reign of God on earth. That Reign of God will be the fulfillment of all their hopes. We Christians believe that this promise of God was realized in Jesus.

Jesus was the full expression of God's steadfast love for us. Or, as the little catechism student said so aptly, "Jesus is God's 'Show and Tell.'" Through his life and teachings, Jesus revealed even more clearly who God really is. Jesus showed us God as one who loves and cares for us. One we can call Father, Abba. God is one who forgives us our wrongs and failings. God desires peace for us. God challenges us to love one another—even our enemies. And God calls us to forgive each other.

Jesus said, "I am the way, the truth, and the life." We go to God through him. We follow the way he taught and lived. That way is distinguished by selfless loving and by total trust in God. Jesus' love and trust were shown most vividly when he surrendered himself to the forces of evil in Gethsemane and was crucified on the cross. Jesus accepted even this great suffering, trusting that God, that Abba, would somehow bring about unimaginable goodness from this horrific event.

And God did. We Christians believe God raised Jesus from death, thus proving that life is stronger than death, goodness is greater than evil, and love triumphs over hate. Sometimes we do not appreciate the full significance of Jesus' resurrection for us. That is why I like what Alice McDermott, a Catholic writer, said about the resurrection: "Being Catholic is an act of rebellion, a mad, stubborn, outrageous, nonsensical refusal to be comforted by anything less than the glorious impossibility of the resurrection of the body and life everlasting."

The rest of the New Testament continues God's revelation. The story of Pentecost, for example, tells us that God is the dynamic Spirit who sends us forth into the world, empowering us to proclaim the good news of the gospel. In his letters, St. Paul encourages the young Christian communities to trust in God, the "anchor of the soul, firm and secure" (Heb 6:19). He raises the question, "If God is for us, who can be against us?" (Rom 8:31).

And finally, it is the first letter of John that encapsulates who God is. "God is light, and in him there is no darkness at all...walk in the light" (1 Jn 1:5, 7). John says repeatedly, "God is love" (1 Jn 4:8). God's love for us binds us to God in a loving relationship: "See what love the Father has bestowed on us that we may be called the children of God. Yet so we are" (1 Jn 3:1). This loving relationship with God impels us to reach out in love to others: "Let us love one another, because love is of God; everyone who loves is begotten by God and knows God" (1 Jn. 4:7).

As I said at the very beginning of this book, when a Scripture scholar was asked, "Can you summarize the message of the Bible in one sentence?" The man replied, "I can do it in two words: Life wins!" That is what hope believes.

God of the Scriptures,
you hear our cries for help
and are moved with compassion for us.
You are present in our human history,
*   in our daily affairs.*
You desire true freedom for all of us,
especially freedom from the slavery of sin.
God of steadfast love,
you are faithful to your promises.
You sent us Jesus to teach us the way
*   of selfless loving.*

You sent the Spirit to empower us
to live joyfully and to carry the good news
to the ends of the earth.
You are the firm and secure anchor of my soul.
I place all my hope in you.
And I believe, in the end, that life, indeed, wins.
Amen.

REFLECTIVE QUESTIONS

1. Is there anything in this reflection that touches your heart?
2. What story, passage, or verse in Scripture shows you most clearly who God is?

SUGGESTED MUSIC VIDEOS

- "El Shaddai," Amy Grant
- "Word of God Speak to Me," MercyMe
- "Wisdom Song," Laura Woodley Osman

7

Hope and Love

To love God is to experience a baffling solidarity
with other people. JOHN SHEA

The virtue of hope walks hand in hand with love. That
is what we saw earlier in Péguy's poem. In this chapter,
we will explore hope's relationship to love from three
perspectives: 1) what are we hoping for? 2) with whom
are we hoping? And 3) how far into the future does our
hope go?

What are we hoping for? When we hope for a better
tomorrow, we are hoping for that better tomorrow not
just for ourselves, but also for our neighbor. This means
our hope goes beyond the concerns for our family, our
neighborhood, or even our country. Hope can certainly

include these concerns. In fact, hope often begins close to home. But eventually hope expands the circle of our love to include the needs of the entire human community. In the words of Sara Maitland, hope "is the springboard… for accepting absolutely our incorporation into each other." An example of this kind of hope might illustrate this point.

In 1948, the all-white government of South Africa established a policy called apartheid. This system, as we know, forced a strict separation of non-white South Africans (a majority of the population) and whites. It inflicted a host of injustices on the non-white population. In time, the non-whites began efforts to end apartheid using demonstrations and strikes. Eventually other countries around the world began to join in their struggle against apartheid. That struggle led to a U.N. embargo and the boycotting of items made in South Africa. I recall the principal of a Catholic high school in Florida at that time telling me, "We cancelled our order for soccer uniforms. They were made in South Africa." By taking this action, that school community was aligning itself with the hopes and dreams of non-whites in far-away South Africa. Such international economic actions played a significant role in abolishing apartheid in 1994.

Hope is ultimately concerned with the common good, that is, the good God wants and desires for all of us. We see God's hope for humanity reflected in God's words to the prophet Jeremiah: "For I know the plans I have for you, plans to prosper you...plans to give you hope and a future" (Jer 29:11). The "you" here is not merely Jeremiah; it is God's entire people.

With whom are we hoping? Hope binds us to others in another way, too. What we ultimately hope for, we know we cannot achieve alone. Hope, therefore, calls us to work with others who share our hopes. In love, we work side by side with our brothers and sisters, doing the hard work of righting a wrong in order to improve the future.

There are many good reasons we need others to help us do the work of hope. Working together is an antidote to loneliness, fatigue, fear, and despair. Working together is power. I have witnessed a clear image of the collaborative power of hope. I live near a large Amish community located in Middlefield, Ohio, and I have seen the Amish building a barn. It is an impressive sight. Dozens of men of all ages descend upon a family's farm on a designated day and work together to build the barn. The women work too, supplying all the good food for the day and tending to the children. Working together, the Amish are able to erect an entire barn in a single day. What an example of the beauty and power of people working together to accomplish some great good.

Even Jesus needed others to help him in his work. When he began his public ministry, one of the first things he did was to gather a group of followers around him. Women too accompanied Jesus, tending to his needs. This "inner circle" supported him and his mission. Later when Jesus sent the seventy-two disciples out, he sent them out two by two, implying, "Do not try to go it alone. You need each another."

How far into the future does our hope go? I remember when my parents became grandparents. As their grandchildren were growing up, I recall my mother saying something like this: "I thought once my children were grown, I wouldn't worry so much about the future. But now that I have grandchildren, I'm still worrying about the future—because that's the world they'll be living in." My mother's love and concern were expanding further and further into the future. Her love used to include mainly her generation and the next generation. But with the birth of grandchildren and then great-grandchildren, her love was being extended forward into time.

When we hope, we do not hope only for the generations we know. We hope for future generations whom we will never live to see. Our hope includes those generations who will be living on the earth long after we have been buried beneath it. This is the bedrock of the whole ecology movement. It says that what we do here today has an impact on the future—either negatively or positively. We try to take positive steps to insure a better tomorrow. So we conserve our natural resources, we recycle, we make environmental decisions based not solely on what is good for us here and now, but what will be good for the human community—in fact, for the entire earth community—in the future.

I have been deeply impressed by one of the practices of the Oneida Indians. Before any major tribal decision, they ask this question: "How will what we do here today affect the seventh generation?" The *seventh* generation! Not merely the third or even the fourth generation, but the seventh—a generation of people none of us will live to see! I often say in my talks and retreats: I think that question should be carved in the halls of Congress!

When we hope, then, we do not hope alone. We hope for others and with others. Hope walks hand in hand with love.

God of Endless Love,
you call us to expand the horizon
   of our hope and our love.
May my hope go beyond
my own little world, my neighborhood, my country.
May it expand to include the entire human
   community
and the entire earth community.
Help me to find others who share my hope,
so that we can work together to make our dreams
   a reality.

May my hope and love
extend to the seventh generation and beyond.
I ask for these graces
through the loving power
of Jesus and the Holy Spirit.
Amen.

REFLECTIVE QUESTIONS

1. Who is included in my hope and love?
2. With whom do I hope?
3. How far into the future does my love go?

SUGGESTED MUSIC VIDEOS

- "Ubi Caritas," Taizé
- "Love Will Hold Us Together," Matt Maher
- "Christ Has No Body Now but Yours," David Ogden

8

Hope's Two Daughters

Anger and Courage

The chief danger in life is that we take too many precautions.

ALFRED ADLER

St. Augustine of Hippo wrote that hope has "two lovely daughters": anger and courage. This chapter will explore hope's relationship to these two entities.

Anger gets a bad press in many religious books. It is often viewed as a negative emotion that is incompatible

with Jesus' mandate to love. Scripture sometimes rein-
forces this negative view of anger. The psalmist says, for
example, that we should give up our anger, for "it brings
only harm" (Ps 37:8). In his letter to the Ephesians,
St. Paul writes, "Do not let the sun set on your anger"
(Eph 4:26). A few verses later, he lists the vices we must
renounce as Christians. At the top of the list is anger.

But anger can actually be a positive force in our spiritual life. It can be our friend. When St. Augustine names
anger as a daughter of hope, he explains why: *so that what
should not be, will not be*. In other words, anger alerts us
to something that should not be, to something that is
wrong, to something that needs to be changed. It often
calls our attention to an injustice. In this sense, then,
anger is perfectly compatible with compassion. In fact,
our anger actually can be an expression of our compassion. As Edward Abbey said, "Love implies anger. The
one who is angered by nothing, cares about nothing."

If we look at some of the social movements of the
past few centuries, we see that many of them began with
anger. Women were angry that they could not vote. In
India, Gandhi was angry at the oppression of his people
by the British. Blacks in the South were angry that the
schools their children were forced to attend were far
inferior to the schools for white children. And non-
whites in South Africa were angry at the grave injustice
of apartheid.

The gospels tell us that even Jesus got angry on a number of occasions. The most obvious example was his encounter with the moneychangers in the temple. On this occasion Jesus did not merely say, "Shoo!" or "Scram!" No, he got a whip and swung it over his head, he overturned the tables and chairs, he yelled, and he chased the moneychangers out of the temple. It was not a pretty sight. What was the injustice that upset Jesus so much? The moneychangers were taking advantage of the poor. They were cheating them—and they were doing their underhanded business right inside the Temple, God's holy dwelling place.

Jesus got angry with the Pharisees several times too. Why? Because they laid excessive burdens on the people that they themselves did not bear. In addition, some of them were hypocrites, pretending to be better than they were. Jesus also reacted with anger against lukewarm living, hardness of heart, self-righteousness, and leading children astray. He even got angry with Peter one day, calling him "Satan."

When we become angry, we must consider the underlying cause of our anger. Does it proceed from selfishness or altruism? Is our anger an expression of hatred or compassion? What is our anger urging us to do—get revenge or right a wrong? Anger can help us overcome our fear so we are able to take action for positive change. Such action often requires courage.

Courage is the second "lovely" daughter of hope. We need courage, says St. Augustine, *so that what should be, will be*. As I said earlier, people of hope are in touch with the imperfect world. This means they have a healthy awareness of sin and evil. They acknowledge that evil resides not only in the world around them, but also in their hearts. This awareness of evil does not paralyze them. It does not make them run for the hills. On the contrary, hope summons them to engage with the imperfect world. It calls them to align themselves on the side of goodness and truth in the ongoing struggle against hatred, violence, selfishness, injustice, and all the other forms evil can take.

To align ourselves with goodness is a commitment we cannot ignore. When accepting the Nobel Peace Prize in 1986, Elie Weisel, a Holocaust survivor, said, "Take sides. Neutrality helps the oppressor, never the victim. Silence encourages the tormentor, never the tormented."

Courage, though, is not the absence of fear. We can be afraid and still have the strength to do the right thing. In her autobiography, *My Life, My Love, My Legacy*, Coretta Scott King tells how afraid she and her husband Martin were as they began to advocate nonviolent action for civil rights. She describes the harassing phone calls in the middle of the night, the threats, the insults, the bombings. One night in particular, Martin was so afraid he could not sleep. He began to think he could not continue his work. That night, sitting at the kitchen table with his head in his hands, he said this prayer:

> Dear God, I am taking a stand for what I believe is right. The people are looking to me for leadership, and if I stand before them without strength and courage, they will falter. I am at the end of my powers. I have nothing left. I've come to the point where I can't face it alone.

At that moment, he said, he experienced the presence of the Divine as he had never felt it before. An inner voice said to him, "Stand for righteousness, stand up for the truth, and God will be at your side forever." This deep assurance of God's presence in his life gave him the courage to press on for civil rights despite his very real fears. It is the same with us. The realization that God is with us gives us the courage, no matter what obstacles we encounter, to work for that better world we are hoping for—that better world God has promised us.

Jesus, you became angry
when you came face to face with hypocrisy,
    self-righteousness, greed, lukewarm living,
    and injustices against the poor.
You aligned your whole self
on the side of goodness and truth and compassion.
You had courage—especially at the end of your life.
In Gethsemane, you were terrified of the death that
    awaited you.
Yet you faced your executioners with courage,
knowing that Abba, Father, was with you.
I ask for your kind of anger and your kind of courage
as I strive to take action for positive change in the
    world today.
Amen.

REFLECTIVE QUESTIONS

1. What do you care enough about to get angry about?
2. Have you ever experienced fear and courage at the same time?

SUGGESTED MUSIC VIDEOS

- "Without Seeing You," David Haas
- "He Will Not Let Go," Laura Story
- "Everyday God," Bernadette Farrell

9

Three Examples of Hope in Scripture

Rejoice in hope, endure in affliction, persevere in prayer.
Contribute to the needs of the Holy Ones. ROMANS 12:12–13

Hope is not merely mentioned here and there in Scripture. Hope is the theme of the entire Bible. Both testaments are filled with anticipation of some good in the future, whether it is the end of the flood, deliverance from slavery in Egypt, or the coming of the Messiah.

Scripture wraps this theme of hope in a predominant image, the image of a journey. Scripture says God calls all of us to make a journey, that is, to move forward to another place. Sometimes the journey is pleasant; other times it is difficult. Sometimes the journey is so arduous we may be tempted to forsake it altogether and settle down where we are or (worse yet) go back to where we were. It is the goal of the journey, however, that keeps us moving forward. It is the goal that also determines how much hardship we will be willing to accept along the way. And it is our longing for that goal that gives meaning and purpose to the journey. That longing is hope.

Sometimes the journey we are called to make entails an actual geographic move. God called Abraham out of Ur to the land of Canaan. God called Moses to lead the Hebrews out of Egypt and into the Promised Land. Other times the journey is more interior, more spiritual. God called Jeremiah to be a prophet. God called Job to greater trust in God's inscrutable ways. No matter what the journey, these individuals (and many others like them in Scripture) were willing to travel because they believed God's promise to them: "I will be with you…I will help you."

We can draw strength and encouragement for our own journey from these hope-filled individuals. Their journeys help us to appreciate the multifacetedness of hope. Although Scripture presents many such stories, I have chosen three to focus on here: Mary, the Magi, and the disciples on the road to Emmaus.

MARY

Mary was called to bear the "Son of the Most High." She embarked on this journey with these words: "Behold, I am the handmaiden of the Lord. Be it done to me according to your word." Mary's "yes" is rooted in humility; she knows who she is, a handmaiden. It is also rooted in profound trust in God, her Lord. Immediately after pronouncing her "yes," Mary sets out on another journey, a lesser one. She travels to her cousin Elizabeth. Our central journey of life is often marked by lesser yet significant journeys or "journeys within a journey." Mary's hope for the future is encapsulated in her beautiful Magnificat. In this prayer, Mary paints a picture of the future as a time permeated with God's mercy and power, a time characterized by surprise and reversal: the mighty will be brought low while the lowly will be lifted up; the satisfied will go away hungry while the hungry will be completely satisfied.

THE MAGI

The story of the Magi is also a story of hope. In a homily on the feast of Epiphany, Pope Francis pointed out some important details about this story. First, he noted that the

Magi did not set out on their journey because they saw the star. No, "they saw the star because they had already set out." It was not the star, but their own "inner restlessness" that prompted them to embark on a journey. The Magi were weary of the way things were. They were especially tired of the kind of kings they were experiencing—kings like Herod. Herod ruled by fear. He employed violence. Everything in his kingdom revolved around him: his power, his safety, his wealth, his way. It is interesting to note that while the three Magi were visiting Herod, they could no longer see the star. His palace was a place of tyranny that blocked out all stars. But as soon as they left his palace, the star reappeared and eventually guided them to Jesus, the newborn king.

The story of the Magi reiterates some of the aspects of hope we have already reflected on. Hope is rooted in our restlessness, in our weariness with the way things are. As we embark on our journey, we may not see very far ahead of us. And that is okay. God will provide "stars" along the way to give us direction. Along our way we will encounter "the ways of the world" that are opposed to the ways of the God who leads us. We must resist the temptation to employ the "worldly" tactics of the Herods of our own day: fear, violence, expediency, self-aggrandizement. Instead, we must embrace the methods of the new king, Jesus: love, gentleness, patience, and forgiveness.

THE DISCIPLES ON THE WAY TO EMMAUS

The story of the two disciples on the way to Emmaus continues the journey motif. They had been on a journey following Jesus. But now he is dead, executed in a most horrific way. So they are walking *away* from Jerusalem and from him. They have made a 180-degree turn in their journey. They had hoped in Jesus, but now all their hope is gone. They are going back to their former way of life, the life they had before they ever met the man from Galilee.

But then a stranger joins them. They welcome him into their company. Through their interaction with him they are gradually transformed. How? Through their openness to this stranger, through their genuine dialogue with him, through their pondering of the Scriptures together, and through the breaking of the bread. Their hope is rekindled: "Were not our hearts burning within us while he spoke to us on the way?" Their encounter forces them to make a U-turn. With great excitement, they head back to Jerusalem to share their amazing experience with the other disciples.

The Emmaus story tells us that we too can be pushed to the brink of despair during our journey. If so, we must continue to be open to life, especially to strangers along the way. We must engage in dialogue with others—those with whom we agree as well as those who do not share our vision or point of view. In addition, we must search the Scriptures and be faithful to the breaking of the bread.

God of the Journey,
you have called me to embark
  on my own personal journey:
my particular and unique life.
Keep me faithful to my journey.
Keep me moving forward,
never stopping and settling down,
  or never turning back.
Help me to be faithful to prayer.
Move my heart for the concerns of others.
Give me stars to guide my path.
May I make the ways of Jesus my own:
love, gentleness, patience, and forgiveness.
And when I grow discouraged,
  bring me back to dialoguing with others,
to searching the Scriptures
  and to the breaking of the bread.
Amen.

REFLECTIVE QUESTIONS

1. Did anything touch you in the stories of Mary, the Magi, and the disciples on the way to Emmaus?
2. Is there another individual in Scripture that you see as a person of hope?

SUGGESTED MUSIC VIDEOS

- "Hail Mary, Gentle Woman," Daughters of St. Paul
- "Be Born in Me," Francesca Battistelli
- "I Can See (The Emmaus Road)," Steve Green

10

Hope and Guilt

*Guilt feelings are the warning bells that call us
to repentance and conversion.* CHRISTINE GUDORF

We often think of guilt in an unfavorable way. We speak
of Catholic guilt, Irish guilt, Slavic guilt as if guilt prevents us from being happy and well-adjusted people.
Years ago I read an article in a Catholic magazine entitled, "Don't Cancel that Guilt Trip." I thought it was a
clever title. I also thought its author made a good point,
namely, that guilt is not always a bad thing. In fact, guilt
can actually play a role in helping us to become happy
and well-adjusted people. The more I thought about it,
the more I began to see a connection between guilt and
hope.

First of all, what is guilt? Psychologists say that guilt is the feeling of regret for something we have done. A sense of guilt begins to develop in a child at the age of three, for that is when a child begins to understand that his or her actions have consequences. There are various kinds of guilt. Our guilt can be relatively minor: I'm on a diet and I ate a piece of chocolate cake. Or our guilt can be more serious: I said awful things to my sister. Or our guilt can be deep-seated: I was unfaithful to my spouse.

Guilt is often accompanied by the sense that I should do something to "fix" what I have done. If the offense is minor and does not affect anyone else, we can simply learn from our mistake, say, "I won't do that again," and move on. But if our wrongdoing has had a negative impact on another, then we might have to apologize and do some work to repair the relationship that has been harmed by our behavior. "Bad guilt" prevents us from moving forward. Instead, we keep wallowing in our guilt, feeling miserable about the wrong we have done. But "good guilt" moves us forward into the future. In that regard it can be a companion of hope.

Why is guilt so important in life? We humans are a social species. Guilt causes us to recognize those times when our actions have been harmful or hurtful to others. In this sense, guilt is beneficial to the human family for it fosters a concern for the well-being of others. It makes us attentive to their needs and desires. It motivates us to build or rebuild loving relationships. The healthier the relationships are between individuals, the healthier the total community.

Guilt also causes us to reflect on our decision making. When we have done something we are not proud of, guilt asks, "What are you going to do about it?" I recall working with a high school boy once who frequently got into trouble. He had few friends because of his short temper and mean spirit. After one such incident in which he was cruel to another student, I sat down with him and, in desperation, I asked him, "Is this the kind of person you want to be?" The question startled him. (It startled me too!) He thought for a moment, and then said meekly, "No, Sister." Then he added, "Help me. I don't want to be this way." His guilt made him receptive to change. He eventually made the decision to get some counseling, which helped him get at the root of his anger while offering him better ways to relate to others.

If we do not think guilt is a vital component of the human person, then all we have to do is think of a person who experiences no guilt. That is precisely the definition of a psychopath: someone with no sense of guilt. Serial killer Ted Bundy, for example, said he felt no guilt even after killing more than thirty people. On a larger scale, if there is no guilt we get Auschwitz, drug pushers, toxic waste dumps, human trafficking, unethical business practices, saturation bombings, and terrorism.

Jesus did not focus on guilt. Many sins did not seem to make him particularly irate. He did not harp on sexual sins. He forgave even those who betrayed him and who crucified him. But there were a couple of sins that infuriated Jesus: hypocrisy and self-righteousness. What do these sins have in common? Hypocrites and the self-righteous see nothing wrong with their suppositions or behaviors. They feel no guilt. In his book *The WOW Factor*, William O'Malley, SJ, writes: "Jesus did not come to hawk guilt; he came to offer freedom." Guilt is often the first step toward true freedom.

In his parable of the last judgment, Jesus seems to be saying that what matters in life is not sexual purity, not obedience to religious law, not human perfection. Rather what matters is our sensitivity to those in need. Jesus even lists some examples of individuals in need (in case we couldn't think of any!): the hungry, the thirsty, the stranger or immigrant, the naked, the ill, the imprisoned. And when we respond with love to their needs, Jesus says, we are responding in love to him. Guilt can provide the initial impetus to loving service of those in need.

Guilt, like hope, urges us to positive action to build a better tomorrow. Another true story illustrates this. A woman went to see her pastor. A few years before, she had had an abortion and she was now obsessed with guilt and unable to move beyond it. The pastor listened attentively and then offered a few suggestions. She could not undo the past, he said. What was done, was done. But now, he said, she could do something for the future. She could help children in some way. Maybe she could help with unwanted or abandoned children. Or she could become a "Big Sister." If these were not possible, then perhaps she could help a friend or family member who was raising children under difficult circumstances. Whatever she decided to do, the important thing was to redirect her energies away from fixating on her guilt to helping someone in need.

And then the pastor said something like this: "Turn what was a negative chapter in your life into the beginning of a new chapter in your life, a chapter focused on love for others." This is exactly what guilt—coupled with hope—can do for us. It can start a new love-filled chapter in our life.

> *God of many chances,*
> *give me a healthy sense of guilt.*
> *When I do something wrong,*
> *help me to acknowledge my failing*
> *and take positive steps to mend what I may*
> *   have broken.*
> *If circumstances are beyond mending,*
> *then give me the grace to let go and move forward.*
> *Help me to grow in sensitivity to those in need:*

the hungry, the thirsty, the stranger,
the naked, the ill, the imprisoned.
And if I should write a negative chapter in my life,
help me to begin a new chapter of life, love,
and hope.
Amen.

REFLECTIVE QUESTIONS

1. Has guilt ever been an impetus for greater love in your life?

2. Is there someone in need who could use your love and attention?

SUGGESTED MUSIC VIDEOS

- "Come Back to Me," John Michael Talbot
- "How Can It Be?" Lauren Daigle
- "We Remember," Marty Haugen

11

Ways to Nourish Hope

How could we tire of Hope?
—so much is in the bud. **DENISE LEVERTOV**

As we have seen, hope is a gift from God. But it demands a receptivity on our part. What are some of the ways we can make ourselves more receptive to this gift God wishes to bestow on us? Or what are some ways we can nourish the hope we already have in our hearts?

As I was writing this book, one of my friends said, "If you're writing about hope, don't read the newspaper!" She was half-joking, but she made a good point.

The news media tend to focus on the negative, on what is wrong in the world. But, guess what? That's their job! One of the main purposes of a free press is to call our attention to things that are not right, not good. By doing so, the media hope to arouse people to action, that is, to do something about an abuse, an injustice, a disturbing trend, a natural disaster, a war.

When I watch the evening news, I can easily get disheartened by all the bad news being reported. At the end of the thirty-minute show, however, the networks often broadcast a more positive and upbeat story—about a young man who collects shoes for children all over the world, about a couple married for seventy years, about military personnel returning from overseas and being reunited with their families, about a small church serving the homeless, about doctors volunteering in places of extreme poverty. I often tell my audiences, read the newspaper, yes. But always remember, the newspaper is *not* a mirror of our world. You might have to plow through a lot of bad news before you find that uplifting story on page thirty-three.

So, the first way we can nurture hope is to look for the good in life, the positive—even in small, everyday situations. Here's an example. My elderly mother used to get upset that my father spent so much time outside in his garden. She had things in the house that needed fixing. She also wanted more of his company. But as she was complaining to me one day, she stopped momentarily and then said. "But on the positive side, I look out the window and I see him out there and I tell myself, 'At least I know where he is. He's not hanging out in some bar. And he's doing something he loves to do.'" My mother was looking for the good in my father (and there was much good to be found in him) in order to help her endure some of his shortcomings (and he had some of those too).

A second way we nurture hope is to hang out with other hopeful people. When I read the history of religious congregations, I am amazed how so many of them began not with a single individual, but often with two individuals—or even more. When St. Julie Billiart, for example, founded the Sisters of Notre Dame in France in 1804, she did not do it all by herself. She was supported every step of the way by her good friend, Françoise Blin de Bourdon. Julie and Françoise needed each other in order to start their congregation—especially when things did not go smoothly. (When you are involved in a worthy endeavor, things do not always go smoothly!) The Sisters of Notre Dame probably would never have become a reality without *both* Julie and Françoise. They leaned on each another to keep their hope alive.

I think this is also one of the main purposes of a parish: to keep hope alive in its members. I know my hope is often nourished by the people in my parish. I am inspired when I see people with walkers or in wheelchairs showing up for Mass every Sunday… when I see the hearing-impaired signing with enthusiasm the songs we sing… when I see parents attentive to their children… when I hear the priest or deacon giving an inspiring and well-prepared homily… when I hear the choir and musicians leading us in beautiful faith-filled songs… when I open the bulletin and read about the parish outreach to the larger community…. When I see all of these things, my hope grows stronger.

A third way to nourish hope is to stay in touch with the wonders of creation. If we are downcast, maybe we need to stop what we are doing and gaze at a sunset. If we are weary, maybe we need to sit for a spell by a pond or lake. If we are discouraged, maybe we need to watch the birds at our bird feeder. If we are disheartened, maybe we need to play with a cat or a dog. John Henry Newman, the great English theologian and Scripture scholar, regularly took a train into London to visit the zoo. He must have found encouragement simply by spending some time with the array of animals he saw there.

I have found that playing with a small child is another way of nourishing my hope. After all, even Jesus made time to play with children. The great Indian poet Rabindranath Tagore has said, "Every child comes with the message that God is not yet discouraged of humankind." If God is not yet discouraged with us humans, then how can I be? When I look into the eyes of a child, my hope rallies. I want to help make the world of the future—the one they will live in—a better place by what I am doing now. In that child's name, I want to commit myself to the hard work that hope requires. I recall the words of Dorothy Day: "No one has a right to sit down and feel hopeless. There's too much work to do."

Another way we nourish hope is through prayer. That topic, however, deserves an entire chapter. But before we reflect on prayer, we will meet two individuals who embodied the virtue of hope.

God of hope,
nourish the hope that is already in my heart.
Help me to look for the good and the positive
in my personal life and in the larger world.
Help me to seek and find other hopeful people
      to be with,
to draw strength and encouragement from them,
and with whom I may share my own hope.
Urge me to stay in touch with the many wonders
      of creation:
sunsets, oceans, rivers, mountains, trees,
      flowers, stars.
Help me to notice and appreciate the vast array
      of animals

you have imaginatively created and who enrich
   our lives.
And finally, help me to make time for children
   in my life,
for they are clear reminders to me
of your steadfast hope in humankind.
Amen.

REFLECTIVE QUESTIONS

1. Have you ever used any of the ways suggested here for nourishing your hope? If so, which and why?
2. Do you have any other ways for nourishing your hope?

SUGGESTED MUSIC VIDEOS

- "Friends," Michael W. Smith
- "Lord of All Hopefulness," Stephen Gwilt (with lyrics)
- "One Spirit, One Church," Kevin Keil

12

Two Hope-filled People

Fred and Erma

Transformed people quite simply transform people.

RICHARD ROHR

In an earlier chapter we looked at several people in Scripture who exemplified the virtue of hope. In this chapter, let's look at two hope-filled individuals who lived closer to our own day: Fred Rogers and Erma Bombeck.

FRED ROGERS

Fred Rogers is best known for creating and starring in the children's TV program "Mr. Rogers' Neighborhood," which aired from 1968 to 2001. How did this gentle and soft-spoken man become such a popular TV personality? To answer that question, let's take a brief look at his life.

Rogers was born in 1928 in Latrobe, Pennsylvania, a town east of Pittsburgh. As a young man, he earned a B.A. in Music Composition from Rollins College in Winterhaven, Florida. In 1952 he met and married Sara Joanne Byrd. The couple had two sons, James and John. In 1963, Rogers was ordained a minister in the Presbyterian Church. He was not interested in preaching, however; he was interested in nurturing children.

Since the 1950s, Rogers had been fascinated by TV. Years later, he said that he went into television largely because he was dissatisfied with many of the TV programs for children. He wanted this "fabulous instrument" to educate children on a deeper level. His underlying goal was to create a program that would help children love and respect themselves.

Rogers began each show by donning his trademark cardigan sweater and his sneakers. He wrote all the music for the show, invited a wide range of guests to appear with him, and addressed, in a gentle way, the real issues children were facing. Often he addressed their fears— such as going to school for the first time or their fear of divorce and death. When a child asked him, "What do you do with the mad inside of you?" he answered with a simple song that taught that feelings are both mentionable and manageable. He said we have a power inside of us to stop when we are about to do something that will not be good for ourselves or for others. That power, of course, is self-control.

In 1969 Rogers began working tirelessly for public funding of children's TV programs. Over the years his own show won numerous awards including four Emmys. In 2002 he was awarded the prestigious Presidential Medal of Freedom. The following year he died in Latrobe from stomach cancer.

Rogers has been praised for the profound impact he had on millions of children and their families. In 2003 the U.S. House of Representatives unanimously passed a resolution honoring "his legendary service to the improvement of the lives of children, his steadfast commitment to demonstrating the power of compassion, and his dedication to spreading kindness through example."

But let's hear from the man himself. Here are just a few of his words:

> "Knowing we can be loved exactly as we are gives us all the best opportunity for growing into the healthiest of people."

"Anyone who does anything to help a child is
a hero to me."

"One of the greatest dignities of humankind
is that each successive generation is invested
in the welfare of each new generation."

"Often when you think you are at the end of
something, you're at the beginning of something else."

ERMA BOMBECK

Humor is closely aligned with the virtue of hope. By
encouraging us to laugh at life and ourselves, humor-
ists help us to keep things in perspective. They also help
us to keep moving forward into the future. One such
American humorist was Erma Bombeck. For over thirty
years she wrote a newspaper column, "At Wit's End,"
that eventually reached thirty million readers in nine
hundred newspapers in the U.S. and Canada. In her columns, she chronicled ordinary life in suburbia, making
millions of people—especially women—smile and laugh
each week.

Erma (Fiste) Bombeck was born near Dayton, Ohio
in 1927. Her father, a crane operator, died when she
was only nine. In elementary school she was an excel-

lent student and an avid reader. In junior high and high school, she began writing both humorous and serious columns for the student newspapers. After high school, she worked for *The Dayton Herald* as a copygirl. Her first journalistic work was interviewing Shirley Temple. Bombeck went on to attend the University of Dayton, a Catholic college operated by the Marianist Priests and Brothers. Her English professor, Brother Tom Price, recognized her potential as a writer and encouraged her to continue writing. In 1949 Bombeck earned her B.A. degree in English and became a lifelong active supporter of her alma mater.

In 1949 she also became a Catholic and married Bill Bombeck. Told by their doctors that they would probably never have children, the couple adopted a little girl, Betsy. In the years that followed, though, Bombeck gave birth to two sons, Andrew and Matthew. As a stay-at-home mom, she began writing about life as she was experiencing it. Soon her career took off. She wrote not only her famous columns, but also made numerous TV appearances. In addition, she wrote fifteen books, most of them becoming best sellers. The titles of her books display her wit: *The Grass Is always Greener over the Septic Tank*; *I Lost Everything in the Post-Natal Depression*; *Wait Until You Have Children of Your Own*; and *If Life Is a Bowl of Cherries, What Am I Doing in the Pits?* In her later years, she wrote a poignant book about children surviving cancer.

Bombeck herself was a breast cancer survivor. But few people knew that, since the age of 20, she had been living with a rare kidney disorder that required frequent dialysis. After complications following kidney transplant surgery, she died in 1996 at the age of 69.

Bombeck has given us many memorable lines about marriage, children, and life in general. Here is a sampling:

> "Marriage has no guarantees. If that's what you're looking for, go live with a car battery."

> "If a man watches more than three football games in a row, he should be declared legally dead."

> "Never lend your car to anyone to whom you have given birth."

> "When humor goes, there goes civilization."

> "When I stand before God at the end of my life, I would hope that I would not have a single bit of talent left, and could say, 'I used everything you gave me.'"

And finally, in a book Bombeck personally inscribed for me, she wrote: "To Sister Melannie, I've made it through life through prayer and a sense of humor—in that order!"

God of children,
help us to invest in the care and education
    of the next generation.
May we find ways of making each child feel
    accepted and loved.
May we welcome others into our lives and
    be good neighbors to all.
Give us the faith to see that what looks like the end
    of something
might actually be the beginning of something new.
God of laughter,
When we are at our "wit's end,"
give us the eyes to see the humor
    in our everyday lives.
Bless us with a ready smile that enables us to keep
    things in perspective.
Help us to see that life comes with few guarantees—
except the guarantee of your presence in our lives
and your love for us that knows no bounds.
During our lifetime, may we use up all the talents
    you have given us
in loving service of our family and our neighbor.
Amen.

REFLECTIVE QUESTIONS

1. What impresses you most about Fred Rogers and/or Erma Bombeck?

2. Do you know anyone currently living who you think is a hope-filled person? What makes you think so?

SUGGESTED VIDEOS

*   "Mr. Rogers' Unforgettable Emmy Award Speech"
*   "When God Created Mothers," Erma Bombeck
*   "Thank You for My Life," Oksana Rus (piano, words, pictures)

13

Hope
and Prayer

*We don't pray to be effective. We pray because
God is God and we are we, and therefore that meeting
is the most important thing in our life.*

JANE UBERTINO

One of the main ways we nourish hope is through prayer.
In this chapter, I would like to begin with an excerpt
on prayer from my blog. Yes, I have a blog. It is called
"Sunflower Seeds: Celebrating Everyday Spirituality"
(www.melanniesvobodasnd.org). I post a reflection every
Monday. You can subscribe to it if you wish—and it is

free! In this reflection, I pose the question: Is praying worth it?

*   *   *

The other morning, as I sat down in my bedroom chair at 5:15 and began to pray, I thought: Is the world a better place because I begin every day by sitting in this chair and praying? Am I a better person because I pray every morning? Does my time in this chair make a difference? Is it worth it?

At first, I am tempted to say *no*. After all, my prayer time does nothing to alleviate the sufferings of humanity, does it? My prayer time does not feed a single hungry child. It does not mend one broken relationship. It does not comfort one tormented person. It does not provide employment for one desperate job seeker. It does not help clean up one polluted river.

I am tempted to think my prayer time might be better spent doing something else, something more tangible, more helpful to others. Like what?

- Like researching some critical problem in the world and helping to come up with a solution.
- Like volunteering somewhere—anywhere.
- Like crocheting afghans for the needy, writing a spiri-

tual best seller, painting a religious icon, composing a love song the whole world could sing.
- Like making tapioca for the two Sisters I live with.
- Or even like cleaning out my sock drawer.

In short, I am tempted to think that my prayer time would be better spent doing *anything* rather than sitting here in silence day after day...pondering Scripture...rummaging through my life for traces of the Divine...trying to speak to a God who sometimes seems so far away or even nonexistent.

But despite these thoughts, here I sit today. It is where I sat yesterday. And it is where I plan to sit tomorrow. Praying. Saying words that sometimes are not even my own. Other times sitting, wrapped in a silence broken only by a chirping bird outside my window or an occasional car going down the street. Why do I persist in praying? Is it merely a habit I cannot break?

No, praying in the morning is much more than a habit (though it is that too). Maybe a little story will clarify one reason I persist in praying every day.

Years ago, during the Vietnam War, there was a man who stood in front of the White House night after night with a candle, often alone. One rainy night a reporter stopped to interview him. He asked, "Do you really think you're going to change the policies of this country by standing out here alone at night with a candle?"

The man replied, "I don't stand out here to change the policies of the country. I stand out here so the policies don't change me."

I really believe that praying makes us more able to withstand the temptations of our age, that is, those policies, practices, and priorities that go against the gospel we cherish and on which we have built our life. Praying anchors our life. It is the engine that impels us to continuously reach out to life with wonder, courage, compassion, and hope. Someone has said that praying is like calling home every day. I like that. Or, in the words of the Trappist monk Thomas Merton, praying is "our daily appointment with Mystery." When we pray we are saying, "God is so important to me, my relationship with God means so much to me, that I set aside time each day to communicate directly with this Beautiful, Incomprehensible, and Beloved Being."

*   *   *

If we want to nourish our hope, then, we keep our daily appointment with Mystery. We connect with the One in whom we have placed our unlimited trust. We commune with the One who is the Source of all Goodness and who wants nothing more than to share this Goodness with us.

In addition to our personal private prayer, we also gather regularly to celebrate the Eucharist. Some have called the Eucharist "the great sacrament of hope." And rightfully so. For when we gather for the Eucharist, we are remembering and celebrating God's great love for us, as shown through the life, death, and resurrection of Jesus. And we are acknowledging that, despite the very real hardships and difficulties of life, despite the struggles we see throughout the world, life is nevertheless a miraculous gift and a precious blessing.

> *Unfathomable Mystery,*
> *I'm here.*
> *If you wish to tell me something,*
>   *I'm listening.*
> *If you wish to move my heart to do something,*
>   *just go ahead.*
> *I'm open, I'm ready.*
> *God, I believe in you, help my unbelief.*
> *I love you, help my lack of ardor.*
> *I want to love others,*
>   *curb my self-centeredness.*
> *I long for a better world, heal my cynicism and*
>   *despair.*
> *I wish to be grateful for all your gifts;*
> *mend my lack of appreciation.*

God, I love you.
And I thank you for the gift of your Beautiful Self
    to all of us,
and the gift of my particular and precious life.
Amen.

REFLECTIVE QUESTIONS

1. Do you "call home" to God every day in prayer? Why or why not?
2. To what extent is the celebration of the Eucharist a way to nourish your hope?

SUGGESTED MUSIC VIDEOS

- "Come to Jesus," Chris Rice
- "Native American Prayer Song," apooka4u
- "Lord, I Need You," Matt Maher

14

Hope, Pain, and Sorrow

There is a sacredness in tears....They speak more eloquently than ten thousand tongues. They are the messengers of overwhelming grief, of deep contrition, and of unspeakable love. WASHINGTON IRVING

The question persists: how can we be people of hope when there is so much pain and sorrow in our world? How can we have hope when babies die, when the elderly are abused, when families are torn apart, when violence becomes a way of life, when millions live in abject poverty, and when our environment itself is in grave danger?

How can we hope when we live with chronic pain, serious illness, or the relentless ache that comes from losing a loved one in death?

Many of us are familiar with Julian of Norwich, the fourteenth-century mystic, who left us her amazing *Revelations of Divine Love*. Her words most often quoted are these: "All shall be well, and all shall be well, and all manner of things shall be well." These words are incredibly consoling; and some would say, they are incredibly naïve.

But it is good to recall the circumstances of Julian's mystical experiences. She did not have these revelations while skipping through fields of buttercups and daisies. She had many of them while tossing and turning on a bed of pain. And her visions of Jesus were not flooded in celestial light; they were often soaked in earthly blood. So when Julian first heard these words from God, "All shall be well," she herself doubted their veracity. She wrote, "I thought it impossible that all manner of things should be well." How could the pain and sorrow of the world be transformed into wellness?

Then Julian asked God about a particular person she loved very much. This person is never identified, but perhaps it was her mother, a daughter, or dear friend. But when she asked if this particular person would be well, the answer she received was, "All shall be well." This loved one of hers would be well because this person was inseparably linked to the wellness of "the all."

There have been times in my life when Julian's beautiful words seemed too good to be true. All shall be well? Really? Maybe that is fine for some far distant future, but what about a pain-filled *right now*? As I write this book, I am grieving the loss of my sister, Mary Ann. She was my only sister and my best friend. Mary Ann was a wife, widow, mother of five, and grandmother of nine. By all appearances, she was in good health—until she got a cough that would not go away. She ended up in the hospital where she learned her cough was caused by blood clots. She had a large tumor in her stomach and extensive cancer in her liver and kidneys. When told of her options, my sister calmly and bravely declined dialysis and chemotherapy. Ten days later she died in hospice surrounded by her family.

The suddenness of Mary Ann's death was hard on all of us. We had no time to prepare for living without her. Shortly after her funeral, I was in bed one night and I started to cry. I wondered, "How could she have been so ill and nobody know it—not her, not her doctor?" I was angry. "If only we had caught the cancer sooner, she might still be alive." Then I recalled the first words my sister said when she realized the extent of her cancer. "It's all in God's hands," she said. These words were not some glib remark. Nor were they a denial of her grave condition. No, these words sprang from her profound faith in God as she came face-to-face with her own mortality. "It's all in God's hands." Was that another way of saying, "All shall be well"?

Our pain and sorrow are not erased by hope. We struggle. We weep. We ask "Why?" We remember too that when Jesus appeared to his disciples after the resurrection, he still bore the wounds in his hands and in his side, indelible markings of the terrible death he had endured. The resurrection did not undo the crucifixion. The wounds and scars were still present, still visible. They were a part of his very identity. But the resurrection transformed those signs of his agony into emblems of glory.

In his book *A New Harmony*, the writer John Philip Newell says he was invited to speak in Oklahoma City a few years after the terrible bombing of the Murrah Federal Building on April 19, 1995. The bombing killed 168 individuals and brought immeasurable pain and sorrow to the entire city and beyond. St. Paul's Episcopal Cathedral is just a block from the bomb site. The explosion that day tore part of the roof off the cathedral and damaged the huge Celtic cross that stood on top of it. The cross was the traditional Celtic cross with an overlapping circle. The explosion ripped off one of the arms of the cross and part of the circle. After prayer and discussion, the congregation decided not to fix the damaged cross. Newell writes, "They chose not to put all the pieces back together again. Rather, they chose not to forget, not to try to smooth over the suffering of their people." The broken cross, now embedded in one of the walls of the cathedral, continues to speak of the brokenness of heart in Oklahoma City. "And it speaks powerfully of the brokenness that is everywhere present, of the parts within us and between us as individuals and as nations." Newell concludes that the broken Celtic cross has now become "a balm for the city's wounds."

We hope, then, not because we are free from pain and sorrow. We hope because we believe our pain and sorrow, like the wounds of Jesus, will be transformed into emblems of glory. We believe that everything is in God's hands. And we dare to believe, "All shall be well."

God of hope,
be with me in my pain and sorrow.
Be with me when I struggle, when I weep,
when I ask, "Why?"
Be with me in my own brokenness,
and in the brokenness present everywhere,
within all of us and between all of us.
Give me the faith that does not deny my pain,
the faith that does not try to smooth over
my suffering
and the suffering of others.
Give me the courage to face mortality
knowing everything is in your hands.

And finally, give me the firm conviction of hope
that "All shall be well...
All manner of things shall be well."
Amen.

REFLECTIVE QUESTIONS

1. Julian of Norwich said, "All shall be well." Do you find her words consoling, naïve, challenging?
2. Do you think that pain and sorrow, tears and questioning, can coexist with hope? Why or why not?

SUGGESTED MUSIC VIDEOS

- "Just Be Held," Casting Crowns
- "Psalm 139 Song: You Carry Me," Patty Felker
- "Diamonds," Hawk Nelson

15

Hope and the Beatitudes

The Beatitudes are the essence, the lifeblood and the beating heart of authentic, ancient and living Christianity. ERIC SIMPSON

Perhaps nowhere else does Jesus give us a clearer proclamation of hope than in his Beatitudes. In this chapter we will take a closer look at Jesus' words.

First, there are two versions of the Beatitudes. Matthew gives us eight beatitudes (Mt 5:1–10). But most Scripture scholars think that only the four he shares with Luke belong to the original Beatitudes. Luke's version is the older one (Lk 6:20–23). That is the version we will use here.

Jesus begins with, "Blessed are you who are poor, for the kingdom of God is yours." Much has been written about that word *blessed*. Some translations, like the *Jerusalem Bible*, say, "How *happy* are you…" But some Scripture scholars object to changing the word *blessed* to *happy*. Rabbi Steven Schwarzschild writes, "*Happy* isn't good enough." He says the word *blessed* means "you aren't lost; you are on the right path the Creator intends for you to be on." He concludes: "Exchanging *blessed* for *happy* trivializes the biblical word. You might as well sum up the whole Bible with a slogan like, 'Have a nice day!'"

So Jesus begins by saying that the poor are blessed, that is, they are on the right path God intends for them and, therefore, are extremely fortunate. The word for *poor* here does not mean destitute. Rather it means powerless, helpless, without influence, overlooked. Jesus is saying the poor in this sense are fortunate because, as Scripture says repeatedly, God favors the weak and the lowly. If we are honest, we realize that, in matters that really count, we all are powerless and helpless. We have very little control over anything—our health, the economy, even relationships. Ultimately, we are all dependent on God's goodness and love.

If we are rich, talented, or powerful, however, we can forget our innate helplessness and begin to live with the illusion of self-sufficiency. This illusion can be truly unfortunate, for it makes us see no need to seek God or to be open to God's strength. This paradox of helplessness and strength is expressed clearly by St. Paul when he wrote, "for when I am weak, then I am strong" (2 Cor 12:10).

The second beatitude says, "Blessed are you who are now hungry, for you will be satisfied." Jesus calls the hungry blessed too, not because hunger itself is good, but (as we saw earlier in chapter 2) because hunger is part of the human condition. We all hunger or long for fulfillment. This beatitude is really asking us, "Do you want God as much as a starving person wants food?" Paul Wadell, a professor of theology at St. Norbert College, describes those who do not have this kind of hunger. They "cleave to wealth and possessions, pleasures and comforts, status and honor, power and influence, or else the endless trivialities with which our culture encourages us to fill our lives." They are unfortunate because they fail to recognize how empty they are. The hungry, on the other hand, acknowledge their emptiness and seek the One who alone can satisfy them.

Then Jesus says, "Blessed are you who are now weeping, for you will laugh." Those who mourn are called blessed not because they have a macabre fascination with death and dying. Rather they are called blessed because, as Fr. Demetrius Dumm, OSB, has said, "they have chosen not to insulate and protect themselves from the pain that comes with loving." When we love as Jesus did, we are making ourselves vulnerable to pain and sorrow. But in this beatitude, Jesus promises that, in the end, we will be comforted. There will be no more tears of sorrow, only tears of joy.

The final beatitude is this: "Blessed are you when people hate you, and when they exclude and insult you, and denounce your name as evil on account of the Son of Man. Rejoice and leap for joy on that day! Behold, your reward will be great in heaven." Those are called blessed who are misunderstood or ridiculed because they have chosen to follow Jesus. They live by his standards and not the standards of the dominant culture in which they live. They have freely renounced the striving for power, control, and influence. This does not mean they cannot hold positions of authority or leadership, but if they do, they view such positions as a means of love and service.

Michael R. Simone, SJ, wrote an article on the Beatitudes entitled "Those Who Bring Hope" (*America*, January 23, 2017). He said: "Naming the poor, the weak, the mourning and the hungry *blessed* was deliberately shocking. Such language requires a firm belief that God's kingdom is on its way." Without that belief, the Beatitudes "are airy platitudes, or worse, condescending justifications of human misery." But belief in the coming of God's reign is precisely what hope is. And hope makes these statements "a promise of salvation."

Jesus delved into the Scriptures to compose the Beatitudes. He used words and images already familiar to the people he was addressing. Simone suggests we might want to search the Scriptures to compose our own additional messages of hope that might speak to people today. You might want to try doing this. Here are a few I came up with:

> Blessed are they who feel ugly and useless; for the God who fashions the lilies of the field will show them their true beauty and worth.

> Blessed are the children held prisoners inside their homes by war and violence; for they will once again fill the streets with their laughter and play.

> Blessed are they who live in overcrowded refugee camps; for God will give them a new home.

> Blessed are they who are lost in any way; Jesus the Good Shepherd will find them.

> Blessed are they who have forgotten how to smile; for God will give them 10,000 reasons to laugh again.

Jesus,
thank you for giving us the Beatitudes.
Help me to live them in my daily life.
Teach me to rejoice in my poverty, that is,
in my weakness and vulnerability,
*   for both can lead me to you.*
Help me to hunger for the Living God
even more than I hunger for my daily food.
Give me the strength to bear the pain and sorrow
that often comes with loving.
And if I am ridiculed or hated for following you,
let me never seek power or control over those who
*   hurt me.*
Keep me on the right path God intends for me.
I ask for these things, knowing full well
how blessed and fortunate I am to be your disciple.
Amen.

REFLECTIVE QUESTIONS

1. Do any of the Beatitudes speak to your heart today?
2. Which of the Beatitudes can you try to live out today? How will you do that?

SUGGESTED MUSIC VIDEOS

- "Blessed Are the Poor in Spirit," The Bowman Duo
- "Christ Be Our Light," Bernadette Farrell
- "Blessed Be Your Name," Matt Redman

16

What Others Have Said about Hope

Quotations help us remember the simple yet profound truths that give life perspective and meaning. CRISWELL FREEMAN

I love quotations. In fact, I love them so much I collect them. I started collecting them while I was a student in high school. Now, these many years later, I have seven drawers in my office filled with 3x5 file cards with quotations on them. Over the years, I have used these quotations in my teaching, retreat work, and writing. I even use them in my prayer.

In this book, I begin each chapter with an appropriate quotation. In this chapter, I have carefully selected quotations that speak directly or indirectly about hope. They come from a wide variety of people. I suggest you read these words slowly and even aloud, pausing between each one. As you do, ask yourself: Do I like this quotation—or not? Do I agree with it—or not? Does it add anything to my understanding of hope?

1. "Trust the past to God's mercy, the present to God's love, and the future to God's providence." St. Augustine

2. "As Christians we are least what we could be when there is fear, and most we can be when there is hope." Justin Welby, Archbishop of Canterbury

3. "The note we end on is and must be the note of inexhaustible possibility and hope." Evelyn Underhill

4. Hope believes in "the ever-present possibility of transformation." Kathleen Norris

5. "The greatest heresy is despair, despair of [humankind's] power for goodness, [humankind's] power for love." Abraham Heschel

6. "Hope is a spiritual and even religious choice. Hope is not a feeling; it is a decision. And the decision for hope is based on what you believe at the deepest levels—what your most basic convictions are about

the world and what the future holds—all based on your faith." JIM WALLIS

7. "Hope is courageous, blessed waiting." FR. DON COZZENS

8. "Never be afraid to trust an unknown future to a known God." CORRIE TEN BOOM

9. "Hope prevents us from clinging to what we have and frees us to move away from the safe place and enter unknown and fearful territory." HENRI NOUWEN

10. A church was having its sign painted. The front had the name of the church, the pastor, and time of the Sunday service. The painter asked, "What would you like painted on the back—the side all the people will see as they leave the church?" The pastor replied, "Hope in God."

11. "Hope is contagious." DR. KENNETH HUTCHERSON

12. "The recovery of hope can only be accomplished when we have had the courage to stop and wait and engage fully in the winter of our dark longing." GERTRUDE MUELLER NELSON

13. "Hope and change are hard-fought things." MICHELLE OBAMA

14. "The future of humanity lies in the hands of those who are strong enough to provide coming generations with reasons for living and hope." *GAUDIUM ET SPES* [JOY AND HOPE]

15. "Not everything can be seen, measured, and photo-graphed. Not everything can be described by geometry

or logic. The unseen God is more real than anything we can grasp with our senses. Faith is betting our life that God is real, that God is powerful, and that God loves us." LAVONNE NEFF

16. "In an unlikely place, unimaginable hope was born." HALLMARK CHRISTMAS CARD

17. "Hope lies in the memory of God's previous goodness to us in a world that is both bountiful and harsh." JOAN CHITTISTER, OSB

18. "When you need hope, find someone who has it. And when you have hope, give it away." REV. TIMOTHY SAFFORD

19. "If I could make a wish, it would neither be for wealth nor might, but for the passion for the possible. I wish for eyes which will stay young forever and which will always glow with the desire to see what God has in store for us." SØREN KIERKEGAARD

20. "Life without hope is an empty, boring, and useless life. I cannot imagine that I could strive for something if I did not carry hope within me. I am thankful to God for this gift. It is as big a gift as life itself." VACLAV HAVEL

God, source of all communication,
I thank you for the wise and inspiring words
of those who have gone before us
or who walk with us on this shared journey of life.
May I heed those words that give perspective
and meaning to my life.
Help me to listen attentively and respectfully to the
words of others.
Help me to speak words that give hope and
encouragement to others.
I ask these things through Jesus, the Word of God,
and the Holy Spirit, the Breath of Life.
Amen.

REFLECTIVE QUESTIONS

1. Did any of these quotations touch your heart? If so, which one(s) and why?

2. Do you have any favorite quotes that have inspired or encouraged you?

SUGGESTED MUSIC VIDEOS

- "The Perfect Wisdom of Our God,"
  Keith and Kristyn Getty
- "God Beyond All Names," Bernadette Farrell
- "Pour Down Like Rain," MercyMe

17

Hope and a Sense of Humor

Laughter is the jam on the toast of life. It adds flavor,
keeps it from being too dry, and makes it easier to swallow.

DIANE JOHNSON

Have you heard these?

- Said the circus manager to the human cannonball:
  "You can't quit! Where will I find another man of your
  caliber?"

- Eve was so jealous of Adam that when he came home at night she counted his ribs.
- If you cross a bee and a lightning bug, you get a bee that can work at night.

A sense of humor is closely allied with the virtue of hope in several ways. First, humor, like hope, sees beyond the here and now. It has a wider perspective on life. This is why we adults, because we have a wider view of life, often laugh at things children say—like this:

- A four-year-old went with her father to see a litter of kittens. On returning home, she excitedly told her mother there were two boy kittens and two girl kittens. "How did you know?" her mother asked curiously. "Daddy picked them up and looked underneath," she replied. "I think it's printed on the bottom."
- A little boy was raking leaves with his father. Suddenly a flock of geese flew over. The father said to his son, "Look at the geese! See how they fly in a V?" The boy looked up and said, "Wow!" Then he asked, "Do they know any other letters?"

Humor, like hope, is linked to humility. Humor reminds us of our limits as humans. It enables us to take ourselves less seriously. We can even laugh at ourselves. Many of us, as adults, laugh at our high school graduation pictures—

the way we did our hair, the clothes we wore. We thought
we were "hot stuff" back then. A little wisdom—often
gleaned later in life—keeps our sense of humor alive.

- Before I had children, I had four theories about how
  to raise kids. Now I have four kids and no theories.
- What's more clever than speaking five languages?
  Keeping your mouth shut in one of them.
- Louis was about to start his first job, and his uncle, a
  successful businessman, gave him a word of advice.
  "The two most important words in business are integrity and wisdom. By integrity I mean that when you
  promise to deliver goods at a certain time, you do it
  no matter what, even if it bankrupts you." Louis asked,
  "What about the wisdom?" Said the uncle, "Don't
  make foolish promises."

Laughter also has the power to build relationships. Some
psychologists call laughter the "social glue" that helps
bind us to each other. A few months before my sister
died, the two of us went to a family-friendly comedy
show. Now one of my favorite memories is sitting next
to her that day and laughing hysterically with her at the
antics and jokes from the stage. Laughing next to her at
that show was as sacred as praying next to her at Mass.

Speaking of Mass, here is something the late humorist Erma Bombeck said once. She was at Mass one

Sunday and a little boy sat a few pews in front of her. He began turning around and smiling at everyone. He was not doing anything more than that. Just smiling. Suddenly his mother yanked him around and yelled at him in a whisper loud enough for everyone to hear, "Stop that grinning! You're in church!" The incident made Bombeck wonder: how did religion lose its smile?

- A Sunday school teacher asked her class, "What was Jesus' mother's name?" A little boy answered, "Mary." The teacher then asked, "Who knows what Jesus' father's name was?" A little girl said, "Verge." Confused, the teacher asked, "Where did you get that?" The girl said, "Well, you know they're always talking about Verge and Mary."
- *Medical terminology:* Artery: the study of fine paintings. Dilate: to live long. Post-operative: a letter carrier. Outpatient: A person who has fainted.

The saints believed in the importance of humor. For three years St. Catherine of Siena was besieged by doubts, demonic visions, and taunting voices. She finally banished them with laughter. As soon as she laughed, Jesus appeared to her. St. Ignatius once said, "Laugh and grow strong." And when St. John Bosco was dying, he was asked what his two favorite books were. He said, "My New Testament and my joke book."

- During the long sermon, one person in the congregation began to pray silently to St. Anthony of Padua (patron of those who have lost something)—so the preacher would find the end of his sermon!

- A couple who had been married for fifty years sat on a train. A young couple got on and took seats in front of them. Occasionally the young man leaned over and kissed the young woman. The older woman smiled and whispered to her husband, "You can do that too if you want." He said indignantly, "Don't be silly. I don't even know her."

- Isn't it a bit unnerving that doctors and lawyers call what they do *practice*?

- Where do forest rangers go to get away from it all?

- Protons have mass? I didn't even know they were Catholic.

Even popes have written about the importance of humor. Pope Benedict XVI said, "By its very nature, Christian belief is *glad tidings*....Deep joy of the heart is also the true prerequisite for a sense of humor, and thus humor is, in a certain sense, the measure of our faith." We could also add that humor is the measure of our hope.

God of glad tidings,
give me a good sense of humor.
Help me to have a wide perspective on life,
one that enables me to laugh even at myself.
May I see all the events of life
   against the backdrop
of your unending love, wisdom, and goodness.
And may my belief in Jesus' resurrection,
strengthen my conviction that, in the end,
death is overpowered by life,
evil is defeated by goodness,
and sadness gives way to everlasting joy.
Amen.

REFLECTIVE QUESTIONS

1. What role does humor play in your spiritual life?
2. What are some ways you can keep your sense of humor alive and healthy?

SUGGESTED MUSIC VIDEOS

- "Joyful, Joyful We Adore Thee," Casting Crowns
- "Dear Younger Me," MercyMe
- "There Is a Joy in the Journey," Michael Card

18

Hope Makes a Difference in Our Life

The one who has hope lives differently. The one who hopes has been granted the gift of a new life. **POPE BENEDICT XVI**

The virtue of hope makes a difference in our life. If we have hope we will think and act differently from those who have little or no hope. In other words, hope shows.

If we are people of hope then we possess the unshakable conviction that God loves us and wants good for us.

This conviction frees us from excessive worrying about ourselves, our families, our communities, our world. The key word here is *excessive*. A certain amount of worry may simply be part of the human condition. But if we have hope, we will not let worry take over our lives. Excessive worry can make us anxious and fearful. It can even paralyze us and thus prevent us from doing the good God is calling us to do.

I am reminded of the *Peanuts* cartoon in which Linus and Charlie Brown are sitting together on a log. Linus says to Charlie Brown, "You look kind of depressed, Charlie Brown." Charlie Brown responds, "I worry about school a lot." In the next frame he says, "I worry about my worrying so much about school." And in the final frame he says, "My anxieties have anxieties!" If we have hope, our anxieties will not have anxieties! We will not be anxious, for we will have taken to heart those words from Scripture, "Cast all your worries upon God because God cares for you" (1 Pet 5:7).

If we have hope in God, then we will be open or hospitable to life. For we believe that the primary way we encounter the Living God is through the "stuff" of our everyday. Therefore, we will welcome people, events, and experiences of all kinds. An image might help here. A person of hope does not live in a house with the door bolted, the windows shuttered, and a doormat that says, "Go away!" Rather a person of hope lives in a house with the door unlocked, the windows wide open, and a bright doormat that says, "Welcome!" Hopeful people know that our God is a God of surprises who can show up on our doorstep at any minute in amazing ways.

In the Book of Genesis, we find just such a story (18:1–15). It tells of Abraham welcoming three strangers into his tent one hot afternoon. He and Sarah go out of their way to serve their guests an extravagant meal. Afterwards, the strangers make Abraham an astonishing promise: Sarah will have a child, a son, within the year. This promise was the answer to the deepest longings of Abraham's heart. That promise was fulfilled when little Isaac came squirming into the world just as the strangers had promised. One can only speculate what would have happened that day if Abraham had pulled the blinds and pretended he and Sarah were not at home! The letter to the Hebrews alludes to this story: "Do not neglect hospitality, for through it some have unknowingly entertained angels" (Heb 13:2). As people of hope, we too have probably entertained a few "angels" in our lifetime.

We remain open to life even when we have had our hearts broken. I once read about a 10-year-old girl who had a pet goldfish. But it died. So she got another one. It too died. Then she got a third one. After the third one died, the little girl wrote this poem:

After my third goldfish died,
I said: I'm through with goldfish.
But I didn't mean it.

That is hope.

A hopeful life is also marked by generosity and service. Hopeful people do not have to be calculating or cautious. They do not have to conserve their giving or hold back their love. They are so in touch with the prodigality of God's love, that they are eager to share this kind of love with others. They remember Jesus' image of the sower who sowed the seed generously with a wide arc. And they recall St. Paul's counsel to "sow bountifully" (2 Cor 9:6), trusting in the One who supplies rich seed for the harvest.

Hopeful people know how to wait. They wait with confidence, because they believe that through the life, death, and resurrection of Jesus, God's promises will come to fruition even if they do not live to see that fulfillment. Hopeful people can afford to take time to listen to others, to be present to them. They are in no hurry. They have come to realize that God's timetable does not always correspond with theirs—and that is perfectly all right.

Another indication of hopeful people is gratitude. If we have hope, what will we be particularly grateful for?

We will be grateful for:

- God's unfathomable love that gave birth to all things and holds them in existence
- God's promises that sustain us through the trials and struggles of the journey
- Jesus' life and teachings that give shape to our desires and deeds
- the Spirit who enlivens and strengthens us to work for a better future
- the people God puts into our lives who accompany us on our journey
- the countless blessings that surround us on a daily basis
- the gift of our particular, unique, and blessed life

God of endless possibility,
I pray that my hope will show
in the way I live my life.
Free me from excessive worry,
and from anxieties that can prevent me
from doing the good you are calling me to do.
Help me to be more open to life,
more hospitable to the people—
especially strangers—
I meet along the way.

When my heart gets broken,
give me the strength to continue the journey.
Give me the patience to wait,
to listen, to be truly present to others, and to you.
I ask for all these things
with a grateful and hope-filled heart.
Amen.

REFLECTIVE QUESTIONS

1. How does hope show in the way you live your life?
2. What are you particularly grateful for today?

SUGGESTED MUSIC VIDEOS

- "All Are Welcome," Marty Haugen
- "Servant Song," Bukas Palad Ministries
- "Don't Try So Hard," Amy Grant

19

Images of Hope

Symbols are the imaginative signposts of life.

MARGOT ASQUITH

I am a visual person. When I am driving in unfamiliar
territory, I do not want printed directions or oral com-
mands instructing me where to go. No, I want a map.
Similarly, after viewing a movie, I can carry an image
with me for days, for years, even decades. From the film
To Kill a Mockingbird, for example, I can still see Atticus
Finch (Gregory Peck) walking out of the courtroom.
Then all the Blacks in the balcony rise out of their profound respect for him. And one of the men leans down
to Scout, Atticus' daughter, and says, "Stand up. Your
father's passing."

It is no surprise, then, that, although I like *words* about hope, I also like *images* of hope. Here are a few images or symbols of hope that speak to me.

THE PURPLE FLOWER IN THE PARKING LOT

I was making a retreat once at a place right on the Atlantic Ocean. Understandably, I was drawn to the ocean when I prayed. But one day, I was praying in the parking lot when I spotted a small purple flower. Now flowers are a dime a dozen, right? But this was no ordinary flower. For she was growing not in a flower bed or a window box, but through a crack in the asphalt! There she was, standing all alone. I saw other flowers just like her growing in a bed of rich soil a few yards away, so I knew where she had come from. Apparently, a seed was carried by a late summer breeze and was deposited into that tiny crack. The seed eventually put down roots and, in Spring, it sprouted. I took a picture of "my" flower, my image of hope. She reminds me that hope can grow in unlikely places—even up through seemingly impenetrable black asphalt. All hope needs is a crack through which to sprout.

THE BLUE AND WHITE MARBLE

When Apollo 17 was on its way back from the moon, one of the astronauts took a picture of planet Earth that has since become an international icon. The photo shows

Earth as a small blue and white orb suspended against a totally black background. Later one astronaut said Earth was like a bright blue and white marble suspended against black velvet. I have a copy of this picture on the file cabinet in my office. When I gaze at earth in this photo, I see no borders, no walls, no individual countries. Rather I see the earth as a single community of beings, interconnected as one. When we hope, we must keep the vision of what we hope for always before us. This picture does that for me.

BAKING POWDER

Another image of hope comes from Sr. Macrina Wiederkehr, OSB. She writes: "I was thinking one morning during meditation how much alike hope and baking powder are: quietly getting what is best in me to rise, awakening the hint of eternity." Baking powder is a lot like yeast, Jesus' own image of the Reign of God. Both baking powder and yeast possess the power to make the dough rise. So too hope can get what is best in us to rise.

SEED CATALOGS IN FEBRUARY

Where I live, we can have some hard winters. Although I like the snow in December, by February I am weary of it. But, when I was growing up, February was when my father would order the seeds for his garden. I remember him sitting at the kitchen table with a stack of catalogs, carefully studying the different kinds of seeds to determine which ones would be best for our area of the country. Then he would fill out the order form, write a check, and put it in the mail. I loved those seed catalogues. I liked looking at the colored pictures of red tomatoes, yellow corn, green beans, white cauliflower, and purple eggplant—all in anticipation of the fresh produce that would be ours in the future. A few weeks later, when the seeds would arrive, it was a happy day inside our house— even if it was below zero outside. For the seeds were the promise of spring. They were hope!

PADEREWSKI AND THE LITTLE BOY

This story, though probably fictional, gives us another image of hope. A woman took her little boy to a concert by the great composer and pianist, Ignacy Jan Paderewski. She hoped the concert might encourage her boy to practice the piano. Before the concert, the mother was chatting with friends and didn't see her boy slip away, drawn by the huge concert piano on stage. He went on stage, sat down at the piano, and began to play chopsticks. The audience was shocked. "Where are his parents?" they muttered. Before the woman could get her son, Paderewski came on to the stage and walked over to the piano. He stooped behind the boy, reached around him on both sides, and began to improvise a countermelody to harmonize with the boy's chopsticks. While the two played together, Paderewski kept whispering to the boy, "Keep going… Don't quit… Keep playing… Don't stop…" We are that little boy, hammering away on the piano, playing our seemingly insignificant song. But along comes the Master, who joins our music to his, while whispering to us, "Keep going… Don't stop… Don't quit." What an image of hope!

SPARROWS MAKING MORE SPARROWS

One day in early spring as I was writing at my computer, I glanced out my second floor window and saw two sparrows perched side by side on the roof of the porch. I watched them for a few minutes. They seemed exceptionally fidgety. That's when I realized what they were about to do: mate. Sure enough, the male hopped on top of the female. At first he had difficulty balancing. He even slipped off a couple of times. But his lady friend was very patient and he was successful in his endeavor. And when they were finished "making love," I clapped! Spontaneously. Why? Because they were making more sparrows! Despite all the toil involved in raising baby birds, despite the presence of all kinds of predators, despite the unpredictability of the weather and food supply, they were making more sparrows! Talk about hope! Later I wrote a poem about this incident. Here's how the poem ends:

I clapped.
Why?
Simply because two little sparrows
got together to make new sparrows,
despite the toil of care,
potential storms,
droughts, cats,
and circling hawks everywhere.

My sparrow poem is a celebration of hope. To me it says,
"Life wins!"

> *Maker of all,*
> *help me to see images of your hope*
> *everywhere: in purple flowers,*
> *pictures from outer space,*
> *in baking powder,*
> *and even in sparrows making more sparrows.*
> *Your son Jesus loved images too:*
> *grape vines, mustard seeds,*
> *wineskins, grains of wheat,*
> *mother hens, lost sheep,*
> *and best of all: wedding feasts.*
> *May the images I hold in my mind*
> *enliven the hope I have in my heart.*
> *May these images strengthen my conviction*

that Life, indeed, wins!
Amen.

REFLECTIVE QUESTIONS

1. Do any of these images of hope speak to you?
2. What other images of hope would you suggest?

SUGGESTED MUSIC VIDEOS

*   "Sparrows," Jason Gray
*   "10,000 Reasons," Matt Redman
*   "Write Your Story with My Life," Francesca Battistelli

OTHER BOOKS FROM

Sr. Melannie Svoboda

Everyday Epiphanies
Rediscovering the Sacred in Everything

This classic collection of Sister Melannie's reflections on everyday moments resonates deeply, helping readers discover God's subtle manifestations in small moments throughout the day. A wonderful book to give and cherish.

128 pages | $12.95 | 5½" x 8½" | 9781585959266

With the Dawn Rejoicing
A Christian Perspective on Pain and Suffering

This spiritual exploration of pain offers encouragement for anyone dealing with suffering—whether physical, psychological or spiritual. Sister Melannie writes from personal experience and includes an inspirational prayer with each reflection.

144 pages | $12.95 | 5½" x 8½" | 9781585956999

Scripture Classics
The Lord Is My Shepherd
Psalm 23

Psalm 23 is one of the most cherished and frequently recited prayers of all times. In the hands of Sister Melannie, its words and images take on powerful new meanings about forgiveness, healing, trust, and much more.

104 pages | $12.95 | 4" x 6" | 9781627851121

TO ORDER CALL 1-800-321-0411
OR VISIT WWW.TWENTYTHIRDPUBLICATIONS.COM

TWENTY-THIRD PUBLICATIONS
A division of Bayard, Inc.